Stories from the Roller Coaster

(of a Faith Life)

Heb. 12:28-29

Stories from the Roller Coaster

(of a Faith Life)

AL AINSWORTH

Cover Design by Angie Zambrano

DEDICATION

This book is dedicated to my wife, Loretta. For most of the crazy adventures in this book, you were right there beside me. You once told me that you hadn't always understood where I have led our family and that you hadn't always agreed with where I've led our family but that you have never regretted following my leadership. Those are the second-most powerful words anyone has ever spoken to me—second only to "I do." I love you.

CONTENTS

ACKNOWLEDGMENTS

To my Lord and Savior, Jesus Christ, the One I trust with control of this roller coaster ride of life.

To my book sponsors, who have made this project possible: Jay & Linda Johnson, Thomas & Paulette Greer, Mark & Mara Sada Foster, Charlie & Lu Ann Plyler, Stan & Wilagene McElhenney, and Allen & Annette Ainsworth.

To all those—named and unnamed—who have played even the smallest of roles in causing my faith to grow.

To my volunteer team of editors, who weren't afraid to offer correction for both my grammar and my tone, at times.

To Josh, Amanda, Jerry, Gay, Mark, Mary Sada, and Loretta, the best small group on the planet.

To the Friday morning breakfast bunch at Hazel's, who kept me connected during a tough time in my life.

To the folks at my part-time offices at Big Muddy Coffee Co. in Hernando and the B.J. Chain Public Library in Olive Branch, who made this writer feel at home.

FOREWORD

Once upon a time...so many a story begins. Great stories capture our imagination, gripping our hearts or moving us to laughter or tears. A well-told story helps us to see through the lens of the narrator. We enter his world, stirred to response while seeing what he sees, smelling what he smells, sharing emotions. In the plot lines of a great story, we begin to see and understand ourselves.

I have the great privilege of serving as a Pastor of Discipleship. My role is to teach, coach, and lead people to follow Jesus. One of the most basic elements of being a Christ-follower is telling others about Him. In my pastoral role, I encourage a simple method for doing so: share your own story then share His story.

For years I honed the story of my own faith journey, making sure to include facts, dates, names, places, emotions, and more... every meticulous fact. In more recent years, I made a very unique discovery: My story was lost in unnecessary details. Not everyone could appreciate the nuances of growing up in Hattiesburg, Mississippi, or could fully grasp the ethos of South 28th Avenue Baptist Church, where Gibbie McMillan was the pastor and the floor of the fellowship hall was covered with green shag carpet.

But many who heard my story could almost instantaneously connect when I shared that "there was a time in my life where I experienced deep loneliness" or "in my teenage years, I learned that you don't have to be alone to be lonely." As I expressed my condition, I perceived people in my hearing saying, "ME, TOO!" Our common experiences bonded us together—storyteller and hearers. These universal experiences help us to identify with one another. I call them "me, too" moments. When I read or hear a great story, there are moments when I feel my pulse quicken and I sense that a part of myself is unmasked. As the storyteller shares his insights, feelings, and perspective, something resonates within me. His anecdote may expose a hidden fear, uncover a painful wound from my past, or even inspire me to awaken a dormant dream. His words reveal my very own thoughts, making me want to shout, "Me, too!"

In getting to know my friend Al Ainsworth over the course of several years now, I find myself moved time and time again by "me, too" moments. These moments spring from our conversations and they leap off the pages of his writings. Often, I experience a charge of joy and relief when reading that someone else has experienced something I have, and I hear myself saying those two superlative, utterly human words: *me, too*. Page after page, I find myself saying I've been there, I've felt that, I understand you... or, more correctly, you understand me! *Stories from the Roller Coaster* is Al's revealing himself through the stories of his life. This type of transparency is not unlike inviting others into your home and saying "I trust you. Come on in. This is who I am. Take a look around. Make yourselves comfortable."

Al Ainsworth is not only a master storyteller but also a storyteller with a mission. His greatest desire is that you will experience significant "me, too" moments on your own great journey of faith. As you follow his faith stories and read of his desire to walk more closely in the footsteps of Jesus, perhaps you, too, will be inspired to say..."me, too."

Scott Hanberry
Pastor of Discipleship
Longview Heights Baptist Church
Olive Branch, Mississippi

INTRODUCTION

The back of the line was safe, an easy place to possess courage that was not yet necessary. As the line moved forward, the activity of the butterflies in my stomach intensified. Still, the line was a place for bravado because I hadn't actually committed to the ride yet. I could still back out if I wanted.

I didn't really want to ride this roller coaster. But I didn't want to *not* ride it, either. This was Disney World, after all. You don't go to Disney World to watch people ride rides. You go there to actually experience the parks and the rides for yourself. And we weren't that family that would be back year after year. This was the first trip to Disney World for my whole family, one on which my mother-in-law had wanted to take us for years. My youngest son was five that year, old enough to enjoy the experience at some level, so here I was with my wife and older two children, waiting nervously in line for the Rock 'n' Roller Coaster.

The tension that I felt between fear and bravery–tightened every time another group clambered aboard the ride and shortened the line–was about to resolve. The next ride would be ours. I knew that we would be slingshot like a rocket into the tunnel through the wall to our right. Past that, well, I didn't know. The ride was completely enclosed, so I couldn't tell ahead of time how high we would climb or how sharply we would turn or whether or not we would go upside down. I think my not knowing was the main reason that when the roller coaster came to a stop in front of us, I swallowed my fear and stepped through the gate to take my seat.

The boldness I had felt in the line had now all but slipped away. Control of the situation had shifted. Though I still left open the possibility that the ride would be as fun and adventurous as advertised, my doubts were nevertheless quite pronounced. The ride attendant came to my car and pulled the safety bar down. Clang! It fastened securely into place. Thick, padded, and resting about chest level in front of me, the safety bar offered a sense of security...and finality. As the attendant stepped away from the last car, so did my last chance to exit the ride. I was locked in.

The lights dimmed and ear-splitting music thundered through the Rock 'n' Roller Coaster speakers. This was really happening. No turning back now. The chant began, first over the loudspeakers, then joined by the riders: "10-9-8-7-6...!"

Some roller coasters begin with a clackety-clack climb to the top of the first hill, giving riders time to adjust to movement and building anticipation. Like so many of the newer roller coasters, however, this one would catapult us immediately into...whatever was inside that tunnel through the wall now directly in front of us. Zero to 60 miles per hour in 2.8 seconds. Any mental adjustments that nervous riders like me needed to make had to be made quickly.

"5-4-3-2-1-Ahhhhhhhhh!!!!!!!"

The spine-jarring launch catapulted us into sudden twists and turns on the other side of the wall, set to the pulsating beat of Aerosmith's greatest hits. All this in what, at first, seemed utter darkness. My eyes slowly began to adjust to the faint glint of light offered by an occasional sign further along the tracks. I could look ahead and see a small dip, an incline just ahead, a sharp turn to the right. I felt the sensation of what I feared most about roller coasters, total inversion. Once, twice, three times I sensed that we were upside down, twice completely upside down and once in a corkscrew. It was all happening so quickly that by the time my brain registered the next movement, we were already in the middle of it. And then through it.

Barely 60 seconds into this adrenaline rush, the ride slowed. And just like that, the ride was over. Now, just like so many thousands before me, I was instructed to please exit the ride.

***

The safety bar in front of me was my very close friend the first time I rode the Rock 'n' Roller Coaster. My knuckles, I'm sure, were white from my death grip on the bar. While others were screaming shouts of joy, I was holding on for dear life. Yet we were all experiencing the same ride. I slowly began to loosen my grip on the security bar in front of me, realizing that it was not my death grip on the bar that was holding me safely in the ride but its grip on me.

I rode the ride a couple more times that day. My experience began to turn from survival mode to pleasure and exhilaration. The ride itself never changed, but my increasing familiarity with it changed my response to its twists, turns, dips, and drops.

I was finally able to do what you see so many people in the roller coaster promotional photos doing: I threw my hands in the air. Tentatively at first and with more abandon later, I learned to actually enjoy the ride. Fun had replaced fear...for the most part. That was a sensation of which I was already aware.

***

I have had a number of life events that mirrored my roller coaster experience. Some were first-time experiences that brought great fear and anxiety. Others seemed familiar because of similar experiences. Still others I approached with audacity to hide the uncertainty lurking just beneath the surface. Occasionally, I have been able to throw my hands in the air and enjoy the ride. But the roller coaster always seems to be the perfect analogy to a life lived by faith.

My life of faith in Jesus Christ began on April 3, 1985. Back then, at almost 19 years old, I had the naïve assumption that the longer I followed God, the smoother my life would become. The topsy-turvy nature of my life would one day become routine. The unexpected would give way to the familiar. This was a simple, comforting worldview that could not have been further from the reality of the next three decades of my life.

***

If you read my first book, *Lines in the Gravel (and 52 Other Re-Told Childhood Tales)*, you know that I lived what most would call a sheltered childhood. Though mine was a childhood filled with fun, it was also safe. I'm not one prone to risks. As a matter of fact, when I was standing in line to ride the Rock 'n' Roller Coaster at Walt Disney World in 2007 at age 41, I had ridden exactly two roller coasters in my life. One was at the state fair in Jackson, Mississippi, when I was a teenager. The other was a kiddie roller coaster at Stone Mountain a few years before my trip to Disney World. When it comes to the roller coaster rides of faith, though, I have ridden some scary ones—at least, for me.

My life plan was to graduate college, coach high school baseball at one school for 40 years, win multiple state championships, and retire having impacted several generations in that community. I would get married right after college and begin the perfect family a few years later. I would one day retire to sit back to enjoy time with my wife, children, and grandchildren and to revel in all that I had accomplished.

A funny thing happened along the way to my dream life. One year into my career plan and already significantly behind schedule on my family plan, I left my first coaching job. Four years later, I changed jobs again. Eight years after that, I left coaching and teaching altogether. Eight years into another career in pastoral ministry, I began a new career. As a writer and speaker, of all things. So to say that the plan that I had concocted for my life didn't exactly work out—well, that would be an understatement.

I have been energized to take some of the steps of faith I have taken. I have been able to see God's hand uniquely preparing me for directions in which He would lead me. To be completely up front with you, though, I will admit that some of my steps of faith have made me wonder why I got on this ride in the first place. Through this book I will attempt to take you to the places of triumph of my faith stories. In order to do that, though, I must take you through the doubts and fears that sometimes threatened the very faith that God was trying to build in me and in my family.

***

My family was spending a long weekend with my sister Lu Ann and her family in Mobile a few years ago. We had attended their church before, and I was very interested in what was billed as a "casual and contemporary" service with its own pastor right there on the same campus as the main service. My sister's family attended the main service but agreed to go with us to the family life center so that we could check out NewSong that day.

I was somewhat disappointed when Pastor Jim Kinder announced that the Sunday on which we attended was a ten-year anniversary celebration of NewSong. Having never attended this particular service of Christ United Methodist Church, I felt like we were intruding on an inner circle type of service. I had no idea how the Lord would use Pastor Jim's message that day.

He began to explain what this on-site satellite was all about and asked those who had been attending for the entire ten years of its existence to identify themselves. Few responded. For the ones who had come later in the decade, he defined what the original vision for NewSong had been. Then, in a defining moment for me, he declared that what we saw before us that day had not always existed as we saw it. He began to speak of decisions made along the way, changes that had been made and the reasons for them, lessons learned, and the process by which the current ministry had adapted to changing needs in the church and in the community.

At one point early in this celebration message, Jim asked each of us to think back to what we were doing ten years earlier. He asked us to consider where we were in our faith walks. I followed along, remembering some major milestones in my journey with the Lord that had taken place during that time span. My mind also began to wander back over the previous decade for my two older children, then in their mid-teens. I thought about their experience in our own church and the process that had made our services what they were at that time. Did they even have a clue as to the "why" behind the "what" of our own church's methodology?

On the way to the car after church in Mobile that morning, I asked my daughter a simple question: "Do you know why we clap after every song at our church?" Ashton responded that she wasn't sure; she guessed maybe to show appreciation for the singers and musicians and the gifts God had given them. I was saddened that a generation had risen up in our church that did not know the answer to that question.

The Lord had done a remarkable work in our church in 1994, and it changed the way that we worship to this very day. Though the stories of the 1994 revival were repeated often in the decade or so following that work of God, time passed and people who were there moved on, replaced by others that the Lord sent to us. Before long, those of us who had been there in 1994 were left to wonder if the new folks had any idea about what they had missed. My daughter's response to my question gave me my answer...at least in my family.

Months later, Ashton came home from a student service and told us an amazing story from the same era that her student pastor had told that day. The story goes that a young mother of two was having some issues with her eyes; in fact, her doctor later told her that he believed the condition would have taken her sight at a young age. Her church small group, though, felt strongly that this was something the Lord would have them join together in prayer against. They did, and the Lord responded by saving the young mother's sight. Her doctor told her that he believed they had seen a miracle.

Ashton was awestruck by the story, repeating it excitedly to Loretta when we arrived home that afternoon. Loretta listened and then responded gently, "Sweetie, that was *me*."

I felt conviction to the core of my being. How could Ashton *not* know *that* story? One of the greatest works of God in our lives, and our own daughter didn't know. This just should not be. I purposed then to tell our family's faith stories, to write them for this generation and, just as importantly, for future generations.

***

Unfortunately, forgetting our stories through the generations seems to be the default for most Christ-followers, though the Word of God gives us deliberate and consistent exhortation to remember to tell them. Consider the psalmist's words:

> My people, hear my instruction;
> Listen to what I say.
> I will declare wise sayings;
> I will speak mysteries from the past—
> things we heard and known
> and that our fathers have passed down to us.
> We must not hide them from their children,
> but must tell a future generation
> the praises of the LORD,
> His might, and the wonderful works
> He has performed.

Psalm 78:1-4 (HCSB)

Like so many other similar passages throughout the Old Testament, God wasn't just reminding Israel to remember His law and His statutes. No, this was a *reminder to remember* His mysteries and His works. They were to do this remembering

7

through the stories they were to tell from one generation to the next as they went about the routines of their daily lives.

Can you imagine growing up as a Hebrew child and NOT hearing the stories of the plagues, the Passover, the parting of the Red Sea, and the crumbling of the walls of Jericho? Adventures like Elijah and Elisha experienced—why wouldn't you repeat those stories generation after generation? What little boy wouldn't revel in the exploits of the shepherd-king David? And who wouldn't be enraptured by the stories of Samson's strength and Solomon's glory? And what about the guy who was swallowed by a fish or the young men whose faith was tested by blazing fire and hungry lions—those accounts had to be told!

Eventually, the unimaginable happened. Israel stopped passing down the stories that best pointed to God. The stories that best reflected the power and glory of God in the face of overwhelming odds gradually stopped being repeated to the succeeding generations. Even worse than the heroic tales being lost through the centuries, the values that the stories contained diminished until they were hardly evident in Israel's people. No wonder this was a nation that did not recognize their Savior when He came to live among them. The stories—the true accounts that served as foreshadowing for His coming had ceased to be told.

Much of the Old Testament is the regrettable account of what happens when God's people forget to tell the stories to the next generation of what He has done. Eventually, His works are forgotten and people are left lacking a higher purpose other than themselves for which to live. Generations suffer because people neglect to tell the stories. There's a lesson in that for our own generation.

I think a significant term needs to be defined at this point. It's a phrase that is the foundation and the centerpiece of my platform as a writer and speaker. Many consider telling the stories from the past as simply nostalgia. They deem others who continually tell stories from the good ol' days as stuck in the past. This is certainly true in some cases. But what I espouse—and what I think God intended through the writers of the Bible—is what I call *values storying*.

Values storying is the passing of values from one generation to the next through the stories we tell...and re-tell. Values storying is not nostalgia; it is legacy building. Whereas nostalgia reaches into the past with both hands to grasp what is already gone and likely never will be again, legacy reaches into the past with one hand to grasp what is teachable and passes it forward with the other hand to the next generation. It is storytelling with a purpose, a purpose that will transcend the lives of those tell their stories into the lives of those who hear them...and repeat them.

***

Think of the stories that make your heart swell with emotion. Good winning out over evil. The underdog snatching victory from the jaws of defeat. The hero riding in to save the day. Stories of redemption. These aren't just the best that movie producers can muster; these are human stories. These are our stories. The best that literature and cinema can produce—and even the best stories we can muster from our own experience—are still a mere reflection of the greatest story every told, God's redemption of fallen man. Just like the children of Israel, though, we neglect to tell our stories.

Maybe we think our faith stories are insignificant. Perhaps when we live a faith story, we just assume that everyone around us "gets it." Or won't "get it." Maybe we don't want to bother others with our stories, or we're just too busy to think back regularly. Whatever the reason—and I've been guilty of them all—our stories of God's work in our lives can gradually fade away if we are not intentional about telling them.

But our stories are important. They matter. On a couple of different levels, they are significant. First of all, faith stories essentially involve the God of the universe entering into His created dimension of time and interacting with human beings.

Secondly, faith stories are the intersection of one human life with many others. Jesus summarized the entirety of the Law into loving God and loving others. This can't happen in isolation. Our stories are essentially connected to others.

I believe that another key principle of values storying is that stories beget stories. If you have ever been around a group of people who began telling stories about any particular topic, you have probably noticed that the first story reminds someone else of a story from his or her experience. Then, someone else remembers a story. And on and on it goes. An intentional ingredient of my writing is to write my stories in such a way as to remind others of theirs. The most satisfying comments that I receive from my readers are ones in which people tell me how my stories remind them of their own.

If I write simply to share my own stories, then my purpose is merely to entertain you. While there is nothing wrong with that, my purpose is a higher one. Throughout the course of this book, I will be sharing many of the stories from my own roller coaster ride of faith. These are stories that both put my faith to the test and, at the same time, strengthened it. The purpose of the book is not that you will necessarily know my stories but that through some of them, you will be inspired, encouraged, and challenged in your own faith ride.

One last important word: I know plenty of people who have much more fascinating stories than any you will find in this book. I can't tell you—like a friend of mine can—what it was like to grow up in three-bedroom trailer that housed 28 people and essentially start my own business by age 11. I can't tell you firsthand like another friend could what it's like to rescue my brother from underneath a mountain of glass. I've never had cancer like other friends, and I've never had a loved one walk out on me like too many others I know.

My stories may pale in comparison to yours—or they may not—but that brings up a danger in sharing our faith stories. We're not called to out-do anyone else's stories but to live the one that God has given to each of us. Read this book with an eye toward the platform God has given you to reflect who He is. Simply allow my stories to be catalysts that help you connect to them. Instead of comparing circumstances, notice the shared Hero of our stories and how the work of God looks so marvelously different in each of us.

When lives of faith intersect, we are strengthened, encouraged, and challenged beyond our own experiences. And we are reminded to tell our own stories. That's the goal of this book.

***

Hebrews 11:1

Now faith is the assurance of things hoped for, the conviction of things not seen.

1 ENTER THE RIDE

Mr. Ron is my friend and a mentor, of sorts. We have had a number of conversations about the times when we realized our mortality and began to feel a sense of urgency about life. He recalls clearly that his mortality moment came on "the day the music died." If someone like Buddy Holly— who seemingly had life by the throat—could be taken suddenly in a plane crash, certainly anyone else could face eternity at any moment, too. I have long admired Mr. Ron as someone who faced retirement without the magical million dollars in his retirement fund and allowed God to teach him another way. I think that much of how he and his wife, Mrs. Judy, serve the Lord now in their retirement years emanated from Mr. Ron's early understanding of man's mortality.

***

I stood shaking at my place at the end of the row. One step to the left would have been all the momentum I would need to begin what seemed a long march forward. But as the final verse of "Just As I Am" faded into silence, the prominent thought in my mind shifted from "I need to go forward" to "I should have gone forward." Conviction turned to regret.

The gospel message was not a common one in our little Methodist church except during our annual summer revival meeting. Visiting evangelists preached with unabated fervor our need to be saved by Jesus. I'm not opposed to evangelistic revival meetings, not by a long shot. Sometimes, voices from outside the norm are necessary in all facets of our lives to move us from the ordinary. George Phillips' message certainly stirred me in that direction on that hot summer night in Star, Mississippi.

This was my night to step across the line into salvation. But I froze. I don't remember how old I was, maybe 10 or 12. A couple of years later, someone in our church noticed that a number of us kids in that age range had not yet been baptized. For the next few weeks, we attended a confirmation class and were baptized in front of the church. I'm sure the class was informative; I remember finally learning the mystery behind our church's staunch belief in the holy catholic church ("universal church," not Roman Catholic Church, as it turned out). However, it was far from transformative.

In the roller coaster analogy that I have established, I was still watching the ride of faith. Though I had been ever so close to stepping from the line and onto the ride, I remained a spectator. In church every week. Family night suppers every fifth Sunday. Vacation Bible school and revival every summer. Community Thanksgiving service every Wednesday before Thanksgiving. Christmas story every Christmas.

Most people I knew back then would have labeled me a Christian, but I was not. I was in one of the most dangerous positions in which someone separated from God could have been.

I was a good person. I minded a great majority of the rules and thought of others before myself...mostly. But at that point in my life, though I believed that God was good and that Jesus died for my sins, I was not willing to relinquish any semblance of control that I felt I had over my life.

***

My world changed on April 2, 1985. That day was a Tuesday, the day after Villanova had pulled one of the most stunning upsets in NCAA national championship basketball history over a highly favored Georgetown juggernaut. I know because I had been talking to my friend Mike about it the night before from my dorm room at the University of Southern Mississippi.

***

Elam Arms was razed a couple of years ago, its destruction long overdue. However, when I chose accommodations for my freshman year of college, it was the only dormitory with semi-private bathrooms. Since communal showers weren't exactly a comforting thought for me, Elam Arms was an easy choice.

Elam also had its own cafeteria, where my suitemates and I could be found every day at 4:45 when the line opened. My family had a large garden, and we would often work until around dark during the summer and eat supper around 8:00 or 8:30. Eating over three hours earlier each night was the first major adjustment I would have to make in college. (By the time my "normal" suppertime rolled around, I was usually ready for a pepperoni and Canadian bacon Domino's pizza.)

My freshman dorm brings back many other memories, mostly centered on my second semester suitemates, Stephen Reed and Steve Keller. They built a bunk bed frame to make use of the vertical space of their tiny room, creating space for a couch, a shelving unit made up of particle-board shelves and "borrowed" milk crates, and a small couch. We spent hours playing Taxi Driver on the Commodore 64, listening to The Police, and making

15

hilarious prank phone calls. Keller's calls to the Kappa Delta sorority, whose members he was convinced had to weigh exactly 100 pounds, were the stuff of legend. They went something like this:

KD phone girl: "Hello, Kay Dee-eee..."

Keller (in feigned foreign accent): "Hello, this is Freddy from Domino's Pizza. Tell Katy her pizza in the lobby."

KD phone girl (Slowing considerably and speaking loudly): "NO, NO, YOU DON'T UNDER...STA-AND. YOU SEE, KAY DEE IS A SUH...ROR...UH...TEE!"

Keller (as Freddy): "OOOOOOOOOOHHHHH! Well, tell her her pizza in in the lobby."

So funny were some of our prank calls that I lament this generation's ability to make them. If Lars down on fourth floor had had caller ID back in those days, we would have been dead men. We almost were anyway. Had the people that we connected using three-way calling known the origin of their calls, they would not have entered into heated arguments about who called whom as we silently listened in. Every sorority would have known that the Pike pledges were not actually the ones forced to sing "De Do Do Do De Da Da Da" to every sorority as part of their initiation.

I was having a great spring semester, so much better than the first. I had tried the whole fraternity experience the first semester—not a good move for me. This "family" that I had been initiated into had threatened to bring me great financial harm upon my exit, but I knew that I could not continue to walk that road. The second semester had been much more fun after I attached myself to my free friends.

The phone call that came from a high school classmate on that Tuesday afternoon in early April, then, came at the best part of my college experience to that point. The news that my friend Mike—still in high school—had died that day of a heart attack on our high school's baseball field was devastating. The next night, after some time at the funeral home and much soul searching, I turned over control of my life to God. I don't remember the words I used or exactly where I was or whom I told afterward, but I knew that I had given over control of my life to God. I had no idea what that decision would entail in the years to come; I just knew that I had a new boss.

***

I wonder if we all have a moment when we are faced with our own mortality. A moment long before we lie on our respective deathbeds. I think we do. King Solomon wrote in Ecclesiastes 3:10 that God has set eternity in our hearts, not so that we would know everything that is to come but so that we would know that there is more to come than just the lives we live on earth.

I stepped across the line into faith while driving home on April 3, 1985. I wish I had answered the call into salvation that night at the little Methodist church in Star those years earlier as the congregation sang all six verses of "Just As I Am," probably even repeating a verse or two. But I couldn't go back and redo the past. I could only step out of the line of regret and onto the ride of faith as an almost-19-year-old and see what it held for me.

If I had seen the twists and turns, the near-darkness, the vertical plunges, and the times to come when my life would turn upside down, I might have stepped out of line again and continued to watch others board the ride. But I would also have missed the exhilaration of a life completely dependent on someone else's control. It's what I call a faith life. There was no turning back from the choice I made on the spring night nearly 30 years ago. No turning back.

***

Galatians 2:20

I have been crucified with Christ. It is no longer I who live, but Christ who lives in me. And the life I now live in the flesh I live by faith in the Son of God, who loved me and gave himself for me.

2 SECURELY FASTENED

When I left my parents' home, I never considered that my life just might not turn out as I had planned. My plan would usher me into success that I would define. I had spent my high school years knowing that I would attend the University of Southern Mississippi, which I did. I would graduate in four years and begin my pursuit of the American dream. Five years later, as I finally reached graduation, my plan was beginning to unravel.

***

My friend David was taking his youth group on a weekend retreat, and he asked me to go along as a chaperone. I had not done much youth group-type work before, but David said I wouldn't need to do much more than just be there. It sounded like fun, and I wasn't doing anything that weekend, so I agreed to go.

I began to learn the value of a spiritual retreat over those few days. The time spent in personal reflection and the emphasis on seeking God pushed me to make some changes that, deep down, I already knew I needed to make. Good intentions had piled high in my life by that point, but I did little to act upon them. I had not grown much at all in my new faith during my next few years of college.

I had not really tried to get off the ride of faith since I boarded it. I just didn't know what to do. I went to church most Sundays, but I never really plugged into one consistently. I didn't know to look for someone to help disciple me, to teach me the basics of my new faith. Though I had been raised in church, I felt lost on this new faith ride. I must admit that some of the most regrettable years of my life came during the few years immediately following the beginning of my new life in Christ.

***

I look back on that tender age in my faith life and see God's grace covering it. I had committed to the ride of faith, for sure. However, I was just sitting on the ride, waiting to see what would happen next. My perspective had changed, certainly. I was no longer just watching others try to live their lives of faith. I was committed; I just wasn't moving much.

Jesus spoke of many certainties of the faith life. Some of those sayings were what drew many of His followers to Him. Who wouldn't want to lay aside the heavy burdens of this life and find rest? Who wouldn't want "living water" and "daily bread" and other promises to the believer?

Jesus told of other aspects of faith in Him, ones that perhaps were not quite so magnetic. He promised that those who followed Him would suffer and that they would be persecuted for His name's sake. Many would be mocked and ridiculed for their faith. Some would be martyred. He did not hide this certainty. I wonder, though: Did anyone who ever shared the gospel with you ever include pain, suffering, and persecution in the package?

Our Western mindsets often tell us that when the Lord securely straps us into the ride of faith through His Holy Spirit, then the faith journey will begin with God's blessings, poured out on us—blessings that we define. We begin to prayer for God to shape us into the people that...we want to be. But what about what *He* wants us to be?

***

I spent the better part of my college years attempting to add God to my life. I had seen Him at work in my life in certain areas. He had answered prayers that I had prayed. However, I was still in the very early stages of learning what it meant to surrender control...especially concerning my life plans.

I was not growing much in my new faith. I went to church most weekends, either in Hattiesburg or back home at my parents' church. I didn't really get involved, though, nor did I get involved with other believers through campus Christian organizations. Looking back on those years now, I have many regrets—not so much for what I did (though there were certainly different choices I wish I had made along the way) but more so for the spiritual growth that I didn't choose to move toward.

***

When it comes to choosing God's plan or my plan for my life— well, I have had to take a few laps around that track. The weekend at the Christian camp in Alabama with David's youth group was one of those times. I wrestled with God, trying to hang on to...what? I wasn't very pleased with the parts of my life that He was trying to pry from me. The hard part wasn't conceding habits and relationships but in relinquishing control.

When I returned from the retreat, David's wife peppered me with questions. She never told me what I should do, but she asked some really good questions that made me say out loud what the Lord had told me. I was nearing a major life change, college graduation, and the time had come to drive a few stakes in the ground.

One decision the Lord was prompting me to make was to break up with my girlfriend of over two years and abstain from dating for at least a year. I can't tell you how I knew God was telling me that other than a deep impression on my spirit during my retreat with David's youth group. Making that step of faith brought me to a crossroads.

In addition to a professional life plan that my college experience was helping me develop, I had a personal plan. I would be married by age 22, begin having children three years later, and complete my family by age 30. And I was rapidly approaching my 22nd birthday. At the end of all my wrestling with God, my choice was still very clear: my way or God's way. I decided to choose His way and not look back.

***

2 Corinthians 5:7

...for we walk by faith, not by sight.

3 MOVEMENT

I need you to understand that I'm not one prone to wait for big signs from the Lord in making decisions. In this case, though, I suppose the Lord did not want to give me any room to miss Him. It was the most exciting ending to any game I have ever witnessed...in my very first game as a coach.

***

I have seen new believers grow in their faith very quickly from the very beginning of their journeys with Christ. This was not the case for me as I have already established, with one huge exception. Shortly after I gave my life to Christ, He led me to what I would do professionally for the rest of my working life. At least that's what I thought at the time.

***

Near the end of my senior year of high school, I had a frank discussion with my high school baseball coach and my school's athletic director. I had always loved sports, and I wondered what a career in coaching might be like. Coach Charlie Butts and Coach Terry Brister both urged me to seek another profession but said that if coaching was in my blood, I would come back to it. Coach Brister told me about a time when he left coaching to work on an offshore oil rig. He made more money than he ever thought he would make, but he was miserable. He quickly returned to the coaching ranks.

I heeded their advice and found a major suitable for my love of sports and my desire to have a financially rewarding career. I would be a general manager for a minor league sports franchise. I saw the general manager of the Double-A Jackson Mets at old Smith-Wills Stadium all the time while attending games there; though he always seemed busy, he also seemed to be having a great time doing his job. I took a junior-level marketing class my freshman year against the advice of the professor teaching the class. I did fine in his class, but the answer I was really looking for was whether or not sports marketing was the career path for me. The answer was no.

Near the end of that semester was when I received the phone call telling me that my friend Mike had died of a heart attack on the baseball field. I turned over my life to Christ, including my choice of what I would do for a living. I prayed for God's unmistakable direction. That answer was not long in coming.

The phone rang later in the semester with answered prayer on the other end. The caller was Coach Charlie Butts, my high school baseball coach. He was facing a dilemma and seeking my help. His son Chris was signed up to play summer baseball in a 13-14-year-old league in Brandon. League officials had added a team at the last minute because of a deluge of signups, and they asked him to coach the team. Not wanting to coach his son until Chris was in high school, Coach Butts asked if I would be interested in coaching the team. I was interested.

***

By my team's first "real" game, we had practiced a few times and played a couple of practice games to prepare for the opening game of the season. I recognized that we had a few good players, but some of them needed a little more time to develop. This would be a good first challenge for me to mold this bunch into a competitive team.

The game started and my career was underway. My team hung in there for a while but gradually slipped to what I believe was a six-run deficit entering the bottom of the last inning. However, one player after another found his way on base until suddenly, we were within three runs and had the bases loaded with two outs.

And up to the plate walked...Reggie. Oh, no. Reggie had plenty of athletic ability, but he had not shown much promise for coming through in this situation—either in that game or in the practice games before it. But Reggie's bat connected on a beautiful deep fly ball to straightaway centerfield, over the center fielder's head! My arm was steadily waving runners to the plate as the ball rolled just under the fence. A ground-rule double would have left us a run short, but the fielder reached under the fence and grabbed the ball to make the throw, keeping the ball in play. I never stopped waving my arm, and Reggie slid into home plate with the winning run on a walk-off, inside-the-park grand slam!

If I was looking for a sign, this was it. I had never before—and I have never since—seen anything like it. Reggie went on to play high school and college baseball, as did three or four of his teammates from that summer team. Another was a star football player at a Southeastern Conference school. And their coach was certain what he would soon do for a living. In changing my major to Coaching and Sports Administration, I discovered that Southern Miss was one of only five schools in the nation at that time to offer such intensive training for high school coaches. It's almost as if someone knew that I would need to be there.

***

I entered the coaching program at Southern Miss at the beginning of my sophomore year, and it seemed exactly where I needed to be. I had a phenomenal student coaching experience at Hattiesburg High during my junior, senior, and second senior years. Those of us who were part of the Coaching and Sports Administration program at the University of Southern Mississippi could earn up to six hours of practicum credit, three for each semester of student coaching. We were encouraged to earn those credits at different high schools, experiencing different surroundings and learning from different coaches. That sounded good, in theory, but in reality it meant that we would essentially have two different experiences as first-year coaches. I chose a different route.

I could not have mapped out a more meaningful student coaching experience. During the spring semester of 1987, I entered into a student coaching practicum at Hattiesburg High School under coach Jim Pierce. That season was the typical first-year student coaching experience: hit some grounders, throw some batting practice, do much more listening than talking in the coaches' meetings. If I had gone to another school for a different experience the following year, I anticipated a similar experience wearing a different uniform. I chose to return to Hattiesburg High the next spring.

My second season as a Hattiesburg Tiger began with exciting news for me as a student assistant. Smokie Harrington Park, a beautiful old semi-pro park that served as our home field, was to undergo some renovations that spring. I came to understand that this was the case every election year as the long-time supervisor wanted to make a splash with voting Tiger fans. The work on the outfield wall was to take place during much of our practice season, though, so we had to make adjustments. The junior varsity team would stay and practice at Smokie, while the varsity would practice at Vernon Dahmer Park a few miles away. This gave me the opportunity to go with Coach Pierce to coach the varsity while his long-time assistant, Robert Worrell, stayed with the JV.

During the weeks-long renovation of our stadium, I was able to serve as the sounding board for coaching decisions for Coach Pierce. Though my role on game days did not change significantly, I learned much about configuring a roster and handling difficult personnel decisions. As I was growing in my knowledge of running a high school baseball team, I also became a more trusted voice, even when all the coaches were in attendance. The season was a tough one, the school's first losing season in quite some time. In many ways, though, the 1988 season was the one that most prepared me to coach high school baseball.

At the end of that semester, I had completed four years of college. I had not quite completed my degree, though. After taking a few classes during the summer, I moved back home to Star to work for a semester with my Uncle Hob before doing my student teaching in the spring of 1989. I could have completed my student teaching during the fall semester, but I wanted the experience of teaching and coaching simultaneously before launching my career.

My third year at Hattiesburg High was different from the other two in many ways. First of all, I was teaching for the better part of the day before baseball practice and going home from practice to grade papers and prepare lesson plans, just like I would be doing when this became a "real job." Second, the school had added a third baseball coach, so I had a little less responsibility than the year before. The biggest difference, though, is the reason I would advocate for student coaches to stay at one school for at least a couple of years. I was no longer receiving college credit for student coaching, but the value of the third year was a mentorship on how to run a program.

Coach Pierce passed on much of what he had learned through the years as he personally invested in my future career—as he also invested in many of my meals that semester. I wanted to do what he had done at Hattiesburg High: find a school with little baseball history but much potential, build a program, win many games, and influence generations of young men over a long career at that same school. With what I learned during my three years at Hattiesburg High School, I felt like I had the blueprint to make my dream come true.

I was also blessed through my student teaching experience at Hattiesburg High School. I was partnered with an inspiring teaching mentor, Mike Tebo. Across 14 years of teaching, including that student teaching experience, I could count on one hand the number of coaches I knew who were English teachers. Coach Tebo was one of them. He taught me that the principles of motivating and equipping athletes to give their best are also very applicable in the classroom. I purposed to work as hard preparing the minds of the next generation as he did.

I completed my student teaching and was set to graduate from Southern Miss on the same day that my sister Lu Ann did. However, one problem stood in the way: our team had a very important out-of-town game with playoff implications on graduation day. I was in Pearl at the baseball game as we won and clinched a playoff spot for the first time in my three years at Hattiesburg. I joined my family back in Hattiesburg that evening to celebrate Lu Ann's and my graduation—though I missed the actual ceremony. I was content with my decision to go to the game. A local sports reporter even included my choice in his sports report the following day.

***

I had a couple of independent study classes to complete before

I would be fully certified as a teacher, and I wrapped those up just in time to pursue a coaching job before school started in the fall of 1989. I was on the verge of all the success I had planned for myself and for the school lucky enough to make me their next head baseball coach. While trying to make that part of my plan a reality, though, I was finding out what it meant to be broke. That was the summer my roommate, Charlie (now my brother-in-law), and I learned to live on the bare essentials. Our third roommate (Stan, also now my brother-in-law) had moved out, and we were left to split the expenses between just the two of us.

I was making minimum wage working at the city park, and Charlie was delivering Domino's pizzas. We were living on pizza and peanut butter sandwiches (because the jelly had run out). When we could muster an extra two dollars, we used a two-for-one steak sandwich coupon at Sonic that the carhops didn't bother to collect from us (allowing us to use it numerous times throughout that summer). Though I was driving a brand new car (because my '73 Comet's engine was on the four-year college plan), the brand new car payments gave me a glimpse of what life would be like if I didn't hurry up and find a significantly higher-paying career. Charlie was in the same situation, so it made for an interesting summer for both of us, one that we still recount often.

***

My first call about a coaching job was from a high school just 30 minutes or so from Hattiesburg. I strongly desired to stay in the Pine Belt area, and this was certainly a school that met my standard of little baseball tradition. As in...none. I met the principal one morning, and he met me with a "dead fish" handshake. His school seemed to have just slightly more life than his handshake, so I returned to my rental house downtrodden. This was definitely not the job for me, and time was running out before school started. I hit my knees in prayer.

Lord, I will go wherever you send me, I pleaded, but I really don't want to go to that school. My answer to that prayer came quickly. The same day, I received another call from the athletic director at Charleston High School.

"Charleston, South Carolina?" I asked.

"No, Charleston, Mississippi," Coach Dean Wright answered.

I was a lifelong Mississippian, but I had never heard of Charleston, Mississippi. I was familiar with most points in the central and southern parts of my home state, but this was new territory. A few days later, I drove up to this small town located at the edge of the Mississippi Delta, about equidistant from Grenada and Batesville.

The fact that the athletic director was late to our scheduled interview because he was tending to his star running back in jail should have been enough to scare me away from this opportunity. However, as I would also realize on a number of succeeding faith moves, when I have prayed and sought God about direction for my life—prayers for His will and not mine—I often sense a counter sense of peace even in the midst of reason. I had a feeling of "right" about taking the job at Charleston.

I laugh now as I think back about the conversation in which I told Coach Wright that I accepted his job offer to be the head baseball coach, assistant football coach, and special education teacher on an emergency teaching certificate (a part of the job description for which I had not bargained). This would be a quick move from my house in Petal to Charleston, and I asked for his assistance in finding a nice apartment there. When I arrived with a U-Haul trailer full of my meager possessions, I found that there were no apartments in Charleston, at least in the traditional sense. My "apartment" was actually three rooms attached to a little old lady's house.

Entering from the back door from where I would park my new Mazda MX-6, the shotgun-style suite consisted of a kitchen, a bedroom, and a spacious den. At $95 per month—and my landlady even paid half of my utility bills—this may not have been what I had in mind, but it fit into my first-year teacher's budget. I still can't figure how I left Charleston at the end of the school year more in debt that when I arrived. I replaced a TV and a VCR, but there was not much to do in Charleston except grab a burger and hang out at Bumper's, so I'm not sure where my money disappeared. This financial lesson was one of many that I learned during my brief time in Charleston.

***

The Charleston Tiger football team of the fall of 1989 was a very talented one, and we were involved in some exciting games. This was a squad good enough to win a state championship if the cards fell just right. They did not, as our lack of a kicker was the difference in a 17-14 loss to Senatobia in the second round of the playoffs. My personal highlight of that season was somehow locking the keys in a running equipment truck after the first-round playoff win at Corinth in the freezing cold. I discovered that Coach Wright was extremely adept with a slim jim and could have easily enjoyed a profitable career as a car thief.

Dean Wright was extremely gritty sandpaper to me during my school year at Charleston. He was very gracious to open his home often to a lonely first-year coach. I became increasingly sullen, though, as his plans for baseball season began to unfold. First, he informed me that I would not be the head coach but his assistant. I was incensed that this man thought he could out-coach me in baseball. He was a fine football coach and, as I was learning, a tough but fair athletic director in a difficult environment. But baseball? No disrespect, but I had cut my teeth in coaching in the Pine Belt, where the best baseball in Mississippi is played. Plus, I had checked out Charleston's results from the prior few seasons, and, well, a change certainly couldn't hurt.

Shortly before baseball practice started, Coach Wright called me over to his house and informed me that I would be the head baseball coach after all, but with one caveat. He would be in charge of my discipline. What?!? I declined fairly politely but inside I had the feeling of a man that, as we say in the South, had been sold a bill of goods. I knew that we had a good group of young men who wanted my energetic leadership in a sport that had been all but ignored in the past. I threw all my energy as an assistant coach into helping them compete and proving myself in the process. But the fuel for that energy was an unhealthy anger.

The baseball facilities at Charleston consisted of a baseball field that had seen its better days. Our one set (as in, the only set) of jerseys was 16 years old. The jerseys had been a bright gold at one time but were sort of a pale yellow by the 1990 season. I had been used to Hattiesburg High, where we wore uniforms much newer than that in practice.

In order to give the Charleston team some degree of uniformity in practice, I purchased a set of T-shirts for the team. Though I had paid for the shirts out of my own pocket, Coach Wright rebuked me in front of the team doing so. I had rationalized that I was buying the shirts to help build the program but, looking back, the fact that I did not include a shirt for him was revealing.

Our baseball team that year won one game. On the last day of school, I drove to my "apartment" one last time to pull an already-packed trailer back to my parents' house in Star. I had already had a discussion with the superintendent of schools and told him of the unfairness of my situation. He offered to work it out where I could coach "over at the junior high." Was he kidding? Had he not read my coaching pedigree? I did not have another job lined up for the following school year, but I knew my time in Charleston was finished.

Less than a year removed from Charleston, I began to see the ugliness of my own arrogance and disrespect for authority. These were traits that would make following God increasingly difficult if they were not broken in me. I have gained more and more respect for Dean Wright over the years, too, as I realize how the Lord used him as the sandpaper on the character of a very rough young coach. He said the things I needed to hear; I just wasn't ready to listen yet.

***

Coach Wright was central to another crucial development in my spiritual development that year, one that I recognized as good for me, even at the time. He invited me to help chaperone a Fellowship of Christian Athletes weekend retreat. Just like the previous opportunity to help with a retreat, the Lord needed to isolate me, to knock me off center and move me forward in my relationship with Him.

The theme of the weekend at Hinds Community College was for the high school athletes to establish a "quiet time" with the Lord, a time each day to read the Bible, to meditate on it, and to listen for God's direction through prayer. I listened intently to each of the sessions, knowing that this was a discipline that I needed in my life. At the end of the weekend, I knew that I was better equipped than ever to live out a life of faith.

I look back to that FCA retreat as foundational to my spiritual growth. I committed to spending time each day with the Lord and have made quiet time a daily practice. The more I move away from the unharnessed young man I was then, the more I recognize God's grace in my year at Charleston. If I had been God or even Coach Wright, I would have given up on me long before that February retreat. But neither of them did.

A few months after leaving Charleston, I listened to an especially convicting message about submission to authority. I made a very humbling phone call to Coach Wright. I asked his forgiveness for my actions and attitudes that I had come to understand had undercut his role as the authority figure God had placed in my life for that season. He was extremely gracious in his response to my apology and was grateful to hear how God had worked in my life during the few months since I had left Charleston. He has now worked as an FCA area director for many years, and God has continued to use FCA in my life, too, even after my coaching career came to an end.

***

The Lord moves in unexpected ways, but He has to get us moving first. Like the beginning of various roller coaster rides, sometimes He moves us slowly uphill, giving us a larger perspective of His plan. Other times, He shoots us very quickly into twists, turns, and loops that He has carefully laid out for us so that we can understand Him and what He expects from us. But we can't attempt to control the ride.

I might think that of all the people on earth who might have my best interests in mind, the best one to control my life would be...me. However, repeated attempts to control my own ride of faith have taught me that when I try to take control of the direction of my life, I lead me toward destruction. Every. Single. Time.

My year in Charleston was one of the most difficult of my life in a variety of ways. I wouldn't go back and do that school year over again, but I wouldn't trade the lessons learned there for anything, either. I had no idea what was next for me, but I knew that I must let God control where He took me, both in my professional life and in all other areas of my ride of faith.

***

Proverbs 3:5-6

Trust in the Lord with all your heart, and do not lean on your own understanding. In all your ways acknowledge him, and he will make straight your paths.

4 SPEED!

The doors opened in the back of the church, and there she stood. My beautiful bride, ready to walk down the aisle to my right. We were moments away from vowing before God, family, and friends to love and cherish one another through every circumstance life would throw our way "until death do us part." My pastor often says that half of the wedding vows are unnecessary. We don't often struggle with the "better" part of "for better or for worse," nor the "richer" part of "for richer or for poorer," nor the "in health" part of "in sickness and in health."

Loretta and I had no idea on June 20, 1992, what crazy twists and turns the Lord had in store for us, though the months leading to our wedding might have given us some indication. We didn't see ahead to the parts of our faith ride that would turn our lives completely upside down. On that day, surrounded by our loved ones, I couldn't believe how fast the last two years had gone.

***

The weekend after I left Charleston, I helped move my sister Wilagene and her husband, Stan, to Tulsa, Oklahoma. While I was there, my brother called with a message that the principal from Hernando High School in the northwest corner of Mississippi had called for me. He wanted to talk to me about a teaching and coaching job there. (In doing the math later, I realized that my application with DeSoto County Schools—submitted when I was first searching for a job and active for one year—would have remained on file for only a few days after that call.)

I interviewed a few days later with Mr. Theron Long, a legendary basketball coach in the area, who was then one of the co-principals at Hernando High. Even though he told me that he had no coaching supplement to offer me, he could offer me a chance to be his school's head baseball coach (the only coach, as it turned out). I would also be teaching English, the subject area for which I had trained. Once again, I knew that this was where God was leading me. And again, I couldn't describe that feeling of just knowing other than an overwhelming sense of peace. I accepted the job and couldn't wait to get to work.

I soon found that my salary would not support rent, utilities, and a car payment in DeSoto County. The Lord provided temporary accommodations, though, with some friends of my parents who had previously lived in Star. Mrs. Peggy Butler worked in the county school office, and she and Mr. James offered me a place to stay for as long as I needed. They lived in Southaven, a larger city about ten miles north of my new school. Within a week of my moving to stay with them, a formative conversation took place.

"Now, Al, you come on and go to church with us this Sunday," Mrs. Peggy stated matter-of-factly in her Duck Hill, Mississippi, drawl. "And then you can go around and visit all those other churches. And then you can come on back and join up with us."

This was a step that I knew was essential for me. I had not regularly plugged into a church since my high school days. Sure, I had attended church fairly regularly, but I had not planted my life in a local body of believers. I wanted to make that one of the first orders of business for my new life in Southaven before other priorities encroached upon my commitment.

***

I went to church with the Butlers on that July morning in 1990, certain that I would "visit all those other churches" but not committing to joining any particular one right away. I couldn't exactly explain what I was seeking in a church, but I had a confidence that I would recognize it when I saw it. That morning at Colonial Hills Church, I knew I had found a home church. I still can't explain exactly why. I just knew.

For the first few months that I attended Colonial Hills, only two people spoke to me on a regular basis. John Arnold was a friend of the Butlers who was about my age, and Jim May was our Sunday school teacher. I naturally assumed all the other young singles had grown up in the church and that it would just take time for an introvert like me to get to know people. Besides, I had plenty to keep me busy.

School started shortly after I moved to DeSoto County, the northernmost county in Mississippi and just across the state line from Memphis, Tennessee. I had a full schedule of English classes for which I had to prepare and a full load of papers to grade. Not long after school started, I moved out of the Butlers' house with their other boarder (a young man about my age) and into a townhouse just down the street.

***

My busyness did not impede my spiritual growth. I had continued the discipline of having a daily time of Bible reading and prayer. I was also attending church every Sunday morning and evening and every Wednesday night. People in our Sunday school class were slowly getting to know one another, as well. We discovered that most of us were just about as new to the church as the others, so we began to hang out regularly outside of church.

I was quite the introvert back then. I would probably still be classified an introvert, but after over 20 years of standing in front of people and teaching in various venues, I'm more of a "forced extrovert" now. I would hang out with the bigger group from church but usually find myself talking to just one or two people most of the night. One night while the group was eating at Pancho's, a local Mexican restaurant, the one person I found myself talking to was a young lady named Loretta.

My roller coaster ride of faith certainly picked up speed after that night. Loretta invited me not long afterward to her parents' home, where she still lived, for Sunday lunch after church. She also invited me to go with her to look at houses...houses for sale and houses under construction. Looking back, I should have run. But I was about as desperate as she might have seemed...if I had bothered to notice.

After a brief hiccup, my career coaching plan was now underway. My marriage and family plan wasn't working out quite like the blueprint, however. When my self-imposed dating hiatus had ended, I didn't find a line of eligible young ladies forming. That's when I met Loretta and ate dinner with her parents and looked at houses with her. My plan was back on track!

Loretta had discovered one of life's secrets that I had not: contentment. As it turned out, she just liked looking at houses...with no ulterior motive. But to a single guy with a marriage and family plan that somehow didn't arrive on the calendar in time, this type of contentment was elusive. I did not seek contentment through my relationship with God or through godly friendships or even through the prospect of marriage itself. No, my discontent came through the fact that my life plan was incomplete in this area. Marriage and family were late to my party.

I have plenty of regrettable stories to tell from my courtship of Loretta. As she and I talk to our kids now about communication with the opposite sex, I am tempted to give examples from the life of "this friend of mine." As tempting as that might be, I must own the embarrassment of reaching in to her car to kiss her goodnight...only later to discover that she didn't want to be kissed! I shake my head and tuck my chin as we tell the story of my telling her that she was "the one" far too prematurely. (I do provide the climax of the story when I tell my kids that I was right....) I was the numbskull who thought it would be cute to correct one of her love notes with my red pen and return it to her like I would a student's essay. And, yes, I was the idiot who once told my future wife after our engagement in early '92 that the thrill of the chase was over.

I look back now to what were still the very early days of my faith ride and see God's hand of grace all over my stupidity. The ride was picking up speed, and I was barely able to keep up with the changes that were happening almost daily in a new town with a new job and a new church and new friends and a new relationship. And new growth in my spiritual journey.

***

The spring of 1991 returned me to the earliest love of my life: baseball. My first season at Hernando began in a very promising fashion with an early-season victory over defending state champion Southaven. Other big wins followed, and our team ultimately won the district championship in thrilling fashion with a walk-off win over Itawamba. We advanced past our first-round playoff opponent before succumbing in the second round.

This was how I had envisioned my coaching career would be. I had a talented group of players who loved the game as much as I did. I had a supportive group of parents who desired a coach who would bring discipline to their sons' team. Feedback from players and parents was all encouraging. I received a number of cards and letters at the baseball banquet following the 1991 season affirming me as the coach for whom they had hoped.

With only three departing seniors, hopes were extremely high for the 1992 season. Players and parents alike were optimistic about our chances for Hernando's first state title in baseball. I did nothing to fetter those hopes and began planning for a state title run.

I would later be grateful that I kept the cards of encouragement from that 1991 season to remind myself of the most enjoyable season I would ever have as a high school baseball coach. Because the joy of my first season as a head baseball coach was fleeting.

**

After baseball season was over, I plugged into a "ministry" of our church in which I felt very equipped to "serve." Church softball was a natural fit for a baseball guy whose playing days had expired. Playing softball also afforded me the opportunity to meet some new people in the church, including some who have become lifelong friends. Two guys in particular, Allen Burchfield and Kevin Womack, made an immediate and lasting impact on my life. Their investment in me ultimately shaped my family's future.

I'm not particularly good at remembering names and faces, and I didn't start out with any existing friendships on the softball team. Allen and Kevin, though, stuck out to me because I had noticed that they sang in the church choir. They worshiped with a passion that I had not yet known, and it drew me to them. They would eventually convince me to join the choir. Even with my biological family's proclivity to avoid singing near others, I enjoyed being a part of the Colonial Hills choir for over 14 years.

Allen and Kevin also persuaded me to join a breakfast group that met at the Southaven Shoney's each week. One of the pastors from our church was walking them through a study of biblical finances. That group became more profitable than any other summer job that I would have through my years as a teacher and coach. I learned about setting a budget and sticking to it, avoiding debt, and generally having a plan for my fiscal resources. That group set the stage for my family's financial future.

**

I had avoided credit cards through my college years, but a trip to St. Louis with Coach Pierce, my coaching mentor, in the summer of 1989 had been too enticing to pass up. I enjoyed the trip and became a Cardinals' fan for life over that long weekend, but I was still paying for the trip two years later. A pair of tennis shoes that I bought while in St. Louis wore out before the payments did. After a year in Charleston in which I should have been able to pay off everything but my car, I was deeper in debt than ever.

By the time I began meeting with my breakfast group, I was several thousand dollars in debt and trying to survive on a teacher's salary with no coaching supplement. I was enjoying my summer break (because that's what my schedule told me I should be doing) rather than working a summer job to cut into my debt. The biggest factor in my participation in the biblical finances group was that Loretta had indicated that my indebtedness would be a detractor in her willingness to move toward a more serious relationship with me.

I began to grasp God's view of money that summer and committed to honor Him with my meager possessions. I began to work my way back to zero. Kevin, who was a vice-president at my bank, worked with me to re-finance my albatross of a car payment to save a whopping nine dollars per month. I was putting to the test the old saying about taking care of your pennies and letting the dollars take care of themselves. I laid out a plan for retiring my credit bills, paying off the one with the smallest balance and snowballing that payment toward the next smallest one.

In the fall of 1991, when most of my debt was gone, I relapsed. Well, sort of. There was this certain small but expensive piece of jewelry that I had been waiting to purchase until the time was right. In November that time had come. With my assurance to Loretta and to Kevin that this was not a step back toward borrowing for everything I wanted, I secured a loan for an engagement ring. Kevin pointed me toward a friend from his hometown who could set a stone of my choice at a fraction of the cost that the jewelry stores in the mall would charge.

Kevin was also the one who told me that this engagement would only happen once, so it had to be done right. He told me the story of his engagement to his wife, Lisa. He had asked her to meet him at their favorite spot in a local park. Shortly after she arrived, he rode up on a real horse wearing a suit of armor. While the knight in shining armor proposal was not my style (largely because of the "real horse" part of the process and my memories of falling from my friend Trey's horse at a kid), I loved the idea of creating a special, once-in-a-lifetime engagement occasion. These are all the rage today but were comparatively uncommon then.

Well, as providence would have it, Loretta and I were asked to play the parts of Mary and Joseph in the Christmas musical at church that year. I concocted a plan and plotted with my co-conspirator to pull it off. Between the Sunday afternoon and evening performances of the musical, I would tell Loretta than our Sunday school teacher had asked us to get some materials for him from our old Sunday school room above the church gym to use in our class's new room. Kevin would run ahead and light the candles that I had set up earlier in the afternoon, and he would be gone by the time we arrived.

As soon as the afternoon performance was over, I made the prepared request, and Loretta joined me—no questions asked, surprisingly—on the walk to the room above the gym. As we neared the top of the steps leading up to the room, I saw Kevin in the corner of my eye in a mad dash around the corner—too late. I lit the candles myself to give light to the flowers just below them, read the love passage from 1 Corinthians 13, and asked Loretta to be my wife. She said yes, and word spread quickly before the evening performance of the Christmas musical that "Mary and Joseph are getting married!"

***

The spring of 1992 was a whirlwind of activity, and my life plan was back in order. I could see ahead to late June, when I would be lying on the beaches of Destin, Florida, with my new bride, basking in the glow of our wedding and a baseball state championship. Yep, that was the plan.

The 1992 version of the Hernando Tigers baseball team had all the requisite ingredients of a Class 4A state champion: two stud pitchers, a line-up with plenty of speed and power, solid defense, playoff experience, and a most important ingredient, hunger. A pre-season statewide #13 ranking let us know that others were noticing, as well. We were ready to take the state high school baseball world by storm.

After a typical early-season rainout, we played our first game on the road at South Panola. They were a great first-game matchup for us, a talented and well-coached squad. It was a game that we should win, but South Panola would not be a pushover. The game went exactly as I would have scripted it...until the last inning when South Panola scored six runs in the bottom of the last inning to steal a victory and knock us out of the rankings for the remainder of the regular season.

The next week was spring break, and I took my team to Hattiesburg, host of the most competitive spring break tournament in the state at that time. The Hattiesburg area of Mississippi has long been home to my state's best baseball. I knew that if we could hold our own in that tournament, that we would be legitimate state title contenders at the end of the season. At the very worst, my team would know how good they needed to be to reach our goal.

The tournament was a homecoming, of sorts, for me. I looked forward to competing as a head coach against coaches whom I had admired during my student coaching days at Hattiesburg. Inwardly, I hoped for a match-up against Hattiesburg High and Coach Pierce. That was not to happen, though, and we left Hattiesburg with a split, two wins and two losses. More importantly, after I suspended one of our players for one game for violation of team rules, dissension entered the ranks of parents and players. I would never again fully have control of the team.

They say that winning cures much of what is wrong with a team. My team returned home from the spring break tournament that year and reeled off 10 consecutive wins. The team was every bit as good as I had thought we might be. Much of our winning streak came in district play, where we were predicted to finish second to newly consolidated Tishomingo County High School from the northeast corner of the state.

I had an ace in the hole when it came to matching up with Tishomingo County, however. A year earlier, before their new school had opened, most of their players were playing for a state championship in Class 2A for Iuka High School. Their opponent was my alma mater, McLaurin High School, and I was sitting in the Tiger dugout to see my school win its first state championship in any sport. However, I was more than a casual observer, collecting data that would keep my Hernando team one step ahead of Tishomingo County throughout the 1992 season.

Sure enough, we captured the division title and entered the playoffs as a top seed. Each round was a best-of-three series, and we quickly dispatched of a very talented Northwest Rankin team with two straight wins. Round two began with a rout of a Louisville. A hiccup in game two set the stage for a do-or-die game three at Grenada High School. My leadoff hitter, in his first game back from an injury, led off the game with a home run, hit another later in the game, and we never looked back.

**

The series win over Louisville set up a North Half championship series with our division foe Tishomingo County. A sports reporter for the *Northeast Mississippi Daily Journal* made his predictions for all of the playoff series and provided all the bulletin board material we would need: "Hernando may have swept Tishomingo County in the regular season, but I don't care if they won a hundred games. Tishomingo County will win this series." Challenge accepted.

Game one was on the road, and it was perhaps the most hostile atmosphere in which I ever coached. The same two pitchers who had squared off twice already got the nod from their coaches to start game one, and they did not disappoint. The game was hotly contested until my first baseman broke it open with a three-run homer to centerfield. It was the only home run of his career and could not have come at a more opportune time.

Game two was a wild, sloppy game played over two days on two different fields because of a rain delay. Tishomingo County held a lead when the game was delayed at our home field. The game resumed at Northwest Community College the following day due to unplayable field conditions at our field. The Braves added to their lead, but my team displayed great resiliency and fought back and cruised to victory, punching our ticket to the state championship round. There, we would take on the McComb Tigers and their undefeated ace pitcher.

We were on the verge of accomplishing the goal for which we had worked so long and so hard. A group of guys who had begun playing together at the dusty old Hernando Civic Center ball fields was now set to take Mississippi high school baseball's biggest stage. And here I was, a second-year head coach, ready to win the first of many state titles for the school. My plan was on track.

We should have been the happiest young men in the world.

***

The suspension earlier in the season had continued to fester in the mind of the player's mother. Though he returned to play a pivotal role in the success of the team, as he had the prior year, she could not move past what had happened earlier in the season. I was later informed that she vowed to "get me," no matter how long it took.

If that weren't enough of a distraction, the inevitable college recruiting began to take its toll on the team. This was one area of the profession in which I had no training and very little direction.

It is also the main part of my time at Hernando that I would do over again if I could.

My two co-ace pitchers were getting the most attention from Division 1 colleges as we neared the finish line of the regular season. My lefty had a knowledge of the art of pitching like few that I have ever been around at the high school level. He could carve up a hitter with a variety of pitches that he would throw at any time in any at-bat. He had studied his craft and was well ahead of most of his contemporaries on the mound. He had a swagger about him that was a major part of his success. I would later discover that it was also the ultimate knock against him with other high school coaches of influence.

My right-hander was the hardest-working player I ever coached. He was still raw as a pitcher but coming into his own on the mound. Also a shortstop, he would not leave the practice field until he had cleanly fielded 10 consecutive ground balls at the limits of his range. He ran the ten 60-yard sprints that all of my pitchers—with one exception—ran at the end of practice with everything he had. I worked hard on his behalf to get the college coaches to pay attention to him, believing he had the "stuff" and the work ethic to succeed at the highest level of college baseball.

The one exception to the pitchers' sprints was the lefty; he had convinced me that we would all be better served by his doing his workout on his exercise bike at home. I was utterly naïve to allow that, but he had earned my trust to that point. He was a top-shelf pitcher, and I didn't think there was any question that he would sign with Ole Miss, his school of choice.

Late in our season, Southern Miss came to one of the games that my right-hander pitched. He pitched well, and they responded with a very nice scholarship offer. Within a week or so, a similar offer came from Ole Miss, and he signed to play for them. The expected offer for my lefty never came. I was shocked and rightly called out for mishandling his recruiting process.

***

46

This was the backdrop against which we would play McComb for the 4A state championship. Frayed relationships between me and several players and parents, as well as divisions among the players themselves, made this a difficult undertaking. But, to the credit of the individuals on that team, they loaded the bus on that Tuesday morning in late May for the long bus ride to McComb ready to compete.

McComb had ridden their star pitcher to victory in the South State playoff series with victories in the first and third games that he had pitched. They had lost game two, but with an ace who came into the championship series with a record of 17-0, they were playing very confidently. All we had to do was figure out a way to beat him once, we thought.

A key home run early in game one would give us that opportunity with my lefty on the hill. McComb, though, clawed back and scored the winning run in the bottom of the seventh inning to take a 1-0 lead in the best-of-three series. We looked forward to facing their now 18-0 ace one more time on Saturday on short rest. We had to win game two first, though.

Game two proved to be a bigger task than we had anticipated. We had two runners thrown out on close plays at the plate, either of which would have given us the win. The game eventually extended ten innings. The call on another bang-bang play at the plate went our way, and we knotted the series at a game apiece. My right-hander went the distance, throwing harder in the tenth inning than he had in the early innings. It would have been the gutsiest pitching performance of any pitcher I ever coached if not for what he did two days later.

***

One game would now decide the state title. When rain threatened the Saturday game at its original neutral site location at Holmes Community College, the McComb coach scrambled to find a replacement field. He did not want to wait until Monday and face the potential of seeing my righty again. I was equally anxious to play on Saturday. McComb's game three starter had pitched with his team's season on the line a couple of times already, and we had worked him hard in game one of our series. Though my lefty was pitching game three on short rest, as well, he had been less utilized throughout the playoffs. I liked our chances.

On Friday before the big game, my right-hander pulled me aside at school and begged for the ball on Saturday. He promised me that his arm didn't hurt at all and that he could beat McComb the next day. I didn't allow his argument to gain any traction and told him I thought we would win without him on the mound. I had to respect his gumption, though.

Saturday finally came, and Delta State University's field was available and dry. Another advantage Hernando, I thought, as we had a much shorter drive than did our counterparts from south Mississippi. This game was not to be a pitcher's duel with crisp defense as the first two had been. We gave up some runs early and by the time I walked to the mound to take the ball from my pitcher, we faced a 6-1 fourth inning deficit.

I did something that day that I wouldn't have done for any other player I ever coached. I gave my game two starter the ball two days after his having thrown ten innings. He just wanted the ball so badly that I couldn't let his high school career come to an end without giving him the opportunity for which he had literally begged. Though his dad had given his consent before the game for him to pitch, if I had it to do all over again, I would not have risked damage to his arm by making the move.

***

If anything symbolized how much fracturing had taken place on our team, that pitching change was it. Allow me quote the thoughtful handwritten card that my left-hander's mother had given me at the awards banquet the prior year. It's a card I keep to remind myself that it wasn't always as bad as it ended for me at Hernando:

"Dear Coach A,

"Thank you so much for all you have done for (our son) this year. You have made a major impact in our son's life. He has really grown up a lot this year. I firmly believe you played a major part in that.

"I also want to thank you for getting me excited about baseball. I really had fun at all the games.

"We are extremely lucky to have a person such of you setting a positive example for our sons. Fondly, ..."

On a sunny Saturday afternoon in Cleveland, Mississippi, the author of that note climbed on top of our team's third base dugout and cursed like a sailor at me with my bride-to-be watching helplessly from the stands. Amongst the expletives, she yelled that I had wanted to remove her son from the game the whole time.

The coach-parent relationship can often be a perilous one, based more on in-game decisions than trust built over time. Believe it or not, what this mother yelled at me that day did not affect me outside of the shock of the moment. I knew that she wanted—expected—her son to win a state championship and be the hero on the mound that day. So did I. Reality can be cruel to our expectations, and sometimes it is easier to lash out in anger than to deal with disappointment. Besides—with a few innings still left to play—the eternal optimist in me decided that I should keep coaching my team until the end...just in case a comeback was in the works.

I would have loved to reason with this mother, explaining that no, I would have loved for her son to pitch us to victory that day as he had so many other times in his career. A shutout or even a no-hitter would have been tremendous. A change of heart from Ole Miss and a full scholarship for him would have made me ecstatic. Regardless of how badly our relationship had soured, he remained one of the finest players I ever coached, and I only wished the best for him. Particularly on a day when he had an opportunity to pitch his team to a state championship.

I look back fondly at every contributor on that team. Their love for the game far surpassed any other team I would coach in the years to come. The pitchers may have gotten the most attention, but they were far from the only talented players on the team. When that team was at its best, they played hard and smart and with abandon. They also had a tremendous amount of fun being teammates. It was heartbreaking to see that eroding over the course of the season and to face the finality of it as we looked up at a five-run deficit.

**

A funny thing happened on our way to defeat on that sunny Saturday at Delta State. My team decided that, no matter what was going on outside the fence, they were going to compete until the very end. We chipped away at McComb's lead, and my right-hander proved nearly as effective as he had two days earlier. Still, we reached the bottom of the seventh inning, our last opportunity, down 7-4. Their big guy on the mound was tiring, and the game was going to be his to win or lose. The question remaining was if he had enough gas left in the tank for one more inning with a three-run cushion.

As the bottom of the seventh inning unfolded, one hit turned into two and then three, and suddenly, we had cut the lead to 7-6. We had a runner at first, still with just one out. Two crisply hit ground balls to the third baseman each led to force outs at second base. Our season was over, one tantalizing run away from our goal of a state championship.

I have a dream every few years, more infrequently as time has passed, where I see the third baseman sailing one of those throws over the second baseman's head. The right-centerfield wall at Delta State is deep, possibly deep enough for two runs to score and change the outcome of the game and the series.

As it was, though, their ace pitcher finished a perfect 19-0 before succumbing to arm injuries before his college career ever gained any traction. My right-hander set the single-season saves record at Ole Miss before being drafted by the Minnesota Twins in the 10th round. My lefty helped pitch Florida Southern to a Division 2 World Series championship. Several others from that team went on to play college ball and enjoyed varying degrees of success.

***

A greater dream than that elusive state championship has emerged over the years. That was the most talented team I ever coached and the one in which I was most personally vested. Maybe I kept a certain distance from others that I would coach in the years to come because of what happened to the relationships on that team. My dream now is for that team to be reunited one day. I haven't seen some of those guys since the day we all cried together out in left field at Delta State. Some of the ones I have seen have not stayed in touch with their teammates, either. That's a shame.

Just a year before our North Half championship season, I had been presented with a very nice framed print with a thoughtfully engraved plaque as a gift from the parents of my team. Following the most successful season in the school's history, I was given a tiny trophy with a baseball signed by the team. Perhaps fittingly, the ball was signed with regular ink pens, and the signatures had all but faded away by the time the next school year rolled around.

***

I did not have long after the season to stew in what went wrong or to re-create scenarios in which we would have come out on top. I had a wedding for which to prepare and a new apartment into which I would move. June 20, 1992, couldn't come soon enough. I'm not sure if I would consider the immediacy of Loretta's and my wedding after a baseball season of heartbreak a blessing or not. Life doesn't always give us that choice. It often seems to move too fast, cruelly sometimes and mercifully at others. (The original date for our wedding was actually June 6, which was exactly one week after our last baseball game. Our pastor's need to re-schedule for two weeks later turned out to be a huge blessing.)

Nevertheless, June 20 arrived right on schedule. My friend Doug proved to be a promise keeper by helping me hide my car at the Memphis hotel where Loretta and I would stay that night without giving up the hotel's location to any would-be "artists." There, a limousine would deliver Loretta and me after the wedding reception. I don't remember much else about the morning of our wedding except arriving at the church on time that afternoon for the eleventy-thousand or so photographs that needed to be taken.

Our pastor, Dr. Steve Bennett, performed our ceremony. I mention that because I would remind him of it during one of the biggest faith moves of our marriage a few years down the road. "Preacher," as he was fondly known, was instrumental in much of my spiritual formation. He would make small talk with me and "Miss Lo-retta" during the non-speaking parts of our ceremony to ease our nerves. He also refused to accept any money for performing our wedding, telling me instead to "take your wife out to a nice dinner on your honeymoon." (Preacher, if you're reading this, I still remember overlooking the gulf and watching the sunset at a nice seafood restaurant with some of the best boiled shrimp I have ever had. Thanks again from across the miles and across the years.)

***

As fast as my faith journey—and my life in general—was moving by the summer of 1992, it froze at the moment the back doors to the church opened and revealed my bride. My heart made a beeline for my throat. I knew that my life would forever change that day, and I was more than ready for it. But just for a moment, time stood still, and I realized what a giant step of faith we were both about to take.

***

Romans 10:17

So faith comes from hearing, and hearing through the word of Christ.

5 TWISTS AND TURNS

The black-and-white tiled floor seemed out of place to me. Really, though, I felt like I was more out of place than the flooring. Walking into our new Sunday school venue seemed eerie and surreal. Our church had recently leased this building less than half a mile from our new church building. This building that was formerly an abortion clinic.

***

Loretta and I were married in the late afternoon and, like many newly married couples, didn't quite find the time during the reception to actually get anything to eat...except for that ceremonial bite of cake, of course. We were starving by the time our limousine dropped us off at the French Quarter Inn in Midtown Memphis. We soon found our way to a nearby TGIFriday's to grab a bite to eat.

When we had finished eating and were walking back to the hotel, a man carrying a baby rushed up to us and offered to sell us the baby. Loretta and I had talked about when we would like to start our family, and a black market baby on our honeymoon night wasn't exactly what we had in mind. As quickly as the man approached us, he was gone again. It was a bizarre experience, for sure, not at all what we expected to happen on our first night as a married couple. This was to be the first of many twists and turns of our journey together.

***

Loretta and I returned from our honeymoon in Destin to our new apartment. She went back to work, and I enjoyed the rest of the summer before returning to Hernando to teach in the fall. It would be my last summer without a side job of some sort.

Returning to school in the fall of 1992 was difficult after the way the previous baseball season had ended. One of the great parts of being a teacher, though, is that every year is a fresh start, of sorts. The halls seemed empty without all my graduated players, but I didn't miss the tension that had filled every day at the end of the prior year.

Loretta and I were just getting settled into the routine of work and school and keeping an apartment when we seized an opportunity we had not been expecting so early in our marriage. Some friends of ours owned both a residence and a rental house in the same neighborhood. They put them both on the market at the same time, intending to live in the one that didn't sell first. We became very interested in the one where their family lived and began to pursue owning our first home.

We qualified for financing for the home and moved toward purchasing it. However, one obstacle stood in our way. We still had six months to go on our apartment lease and couldn't afford to pay both rent and a house payment. We talked to the apartment manager and were told that if they could fill the vacancy, we wouldn't have to pay the rent; we would only forfeit our security deposit. That sounded fair to us, and we began to pray that God would bring a new tenant at a most difficult time of year.

During the Thanksgiving weekend of 1992, we took ownership of our first home. We initiated a whirlwind of cleaning, painting, and moving that first weekend, and we settled into the house. In the meantime a young man and his wife were preparing to graduate from Ole Miss, get married, and move into an apartment in Southaven. He planned to move in first so that they could get the majority of their belongings moved in before the wedding. They found the perfect apartment, our old one, and we were relieved of six months' rent. (Many months later, a check for our security deposit arrived—unannounced and unexpected but very welcomed.)

Our new home was one block away from our church. This was very convenient because we were spending several hours a week there, growing in our faith and in our relationships with others. Little did we know that the most paradigm-shifting time of our lives was just around the corner, as well.

***

When spring rolled around and baseball started, our team experienced a maddening up-and-down journey. One day, we would beat one of our opponents in dominating fashion before losing to a similar team a day or two later. We stayed in the playoff chase for much of the year but fell just short of making the post-season.

I learned that many of the younger players did not have the

love for baseball that their predecessors did and that I did. Frustratingly, I also learned that I did not have the capacity to give them that love and intensity for the game. Some of the negative effects of the 1992 season carried over to the 1993 team, but the positive aspects of winning of North Mississippi championship and coming within a run of the state title dissipated more quickly. Though a 13-11 record kept alive one of my ambitions as a head coach—to never have a losing record—the season was merely average in every sense of the word.

***

Summer brought the first of many seasonal jobs and more movement toward Loretta's and my goal of becoming debt free. I (We) had paid off her engagement ring, and we had cleared all the balances on our credit cards. All that remained was my car payment, and the months were quickly clicking away toward the last one of those. By the end of 1993, we had started a savings account with a little over $500. It wouldn't be there long.

***

The winter of 1993 also brought exciting news to Loretta and me and our families. We were going to have a baby. I had in my mind that I would have a son first, that we would name him Michael, and that he would take care of a younger sister or brother in what we planned to one day be a family of four. Looking back, I should have known that my plans would not be what the Lord had in store for us. As with so many of the other plans that I had made for myself and for my family, my plans weren't necessarily bad; they were just different from God's plans for us.

Our due date was July 4, 1994, my aunt's birthday and a date conveniently nestled between baseball season and my return to school. Perfect. During semester exams for the fall term—just a couple of months into Loretta's pregnancy—I received a phone call at school from her. Before the days of cell phones, a call from Loretta while I was at school was unusual. She was bleeding and needed to go to the doctor to be sure everything was okay.

I remember how kind Mrs. Cheryl Ward, our school's testing clerk, was on that day. I quickly gave her instructions for administering the remainder of my exams that day and raced toward the doctor's office. I prayed frantically, not really knowing what this situation could hold for us and for our baby.

Loretta and I waited fearfully as the ultrasound technician waved the magic wand over Loretta's stomach. We were listening for any positive indication, but she remained silent as she searched for a heartbeat. After what seemed an eternity, she turned to my wife and said, "I'm sorry..." I'm sure there was more information that came after that, but those two words told us all we needed to know. We had lost our child.

This was not a situation that we had covered in our pre-marital counseling. The sadness that enveloped both of us was palpable. I had no idea how to lead my wife through this. I would ask Loretta if she needed to get out of the house, and she didn't know. I would ask her if she just wanted to stay home, and she didn't know. I wanted to help so badly, but neither of us knew what to do.

Miscarriages were not commonly discussed in those days. We knew of one other person, one of Loretta's best friends from high school, who had miscarried. Kim and her family had just moved that weekend. All we knew was the name of the neighborhood across the county where they had moved. No phone number. No address. And no way to readily reach out to them. Just the name of the subdivision: Eastover—only one of the largest subdivisions in our county. Trying to find them would be like trying to find the proverbial needle in a haystack. To add even the stress of not being able to find Kim's house would have been too much. So we stared at the walls.

I cried out to God in my helplessness to show me what to do. So many times, when our first instinct is to *do* something, the Lord just wants us to come to Him, release our burdens, and abide in Him. This prayer, though, led to a one-word instruction. Drive.

So we drove. I didn't know where we would go, exactly. We just drove and drove and drove. Eventually, we drove to Olive Branch and turned on one of the streets leading into Eastover subdivision. Within just a few houses, we saw Larry and Kim's van staring at us from their driveway. Of course! Now that we were a tiny bit above the fog that we had both been under, it made sense. If they had just moved, the garage would be full of unpacked belongings. It seemed intuitive...now...that there would be no room in the garage for the van. Thank You, Lord.

Kim was home and welcomed us quickly into their home. Their little girl Kendall was about three years old, and she would probably have had many questions regarding what were soon to be two crying women, so I asked her if she would like to read me a book. She did, and we went to another room to engage in *Little Red Riding Hood*. Over 20 years later, I still remember Kendall's version: "All the better to *see* you with, my dear....All the better to *eat* you with, my dear." Funny, the next time I saw Kendall was 15 years later on a mission trip to Seattle for which our churches joined forces. She claimed to still remember reading to me, too.

I never asked for specifics about Loretta's conversation with Kim. All I know is that the Lord had provided comfort for my wife through the same comfort with which He had comforted Kim a few years earlier. He had lifted her from what felt like the beginning of a deep, dark place and given us hope.

I learned that day that the Lord is my strength, my hope when all seems lost. Oh, I already knew that, but the lesson dropped from my head to my heart. I also learned that when I feel totally helpless and feel like my last option has been exhausted, He still has resources I can't even imagine. The ride of faith that day involved just one simple step of obedience on my part: drive. I didn't need to know where I would go or what I would do when I arrived there. My instructions were simply for Loretta and I to get in the car and go. He did the rest.

***

Our church had scheduled a men's retreat for January of 1994. I was there along with most of my growing circle of friends. I remember that Allen Burchfield had just moved away and that he came back to go to the retreat. We sat with our mutual friend David Martin and listened to a missionary from Africa. He was a little guy who constantly bounced up and down as he told stories from the mission field on the other side of the world.

Early into the retreat, God began to reveal to all of us that this was no ordinary men's event. When revival comes, its onset can always be marked by brokenness and repentance. As a holy God made Himself known to us on that Friday night, we could hear the pop-pop-pop of theater-style seats of men from all over the auditorium who were making their way to the altars. To be more precise, most of the men who made their way forward to confess sin and ask forgiveness never made it to the crowded altars. They just stopped in the aisle as close as they could get to the front and dropped to their knees.

Our missionary speaker related story after story from the work God was doing in the part of Africa where his family served. God showed us men a different way to live, a way that was sold out to Him and the Kingdom work He wanted to do through us. Up to that point, we were a very typical Southern Baptist church, and our men were not in the habit of singing loudly, confessing sin easily, or displaying emotion freely. That had changed by early Saturday afternoon when the men's retreat came to a close.

Many strongholds were broken that weekend. Men made commitments that would be life changing to their families. One man felt convicted about the alcohol he sold in his store. By Saturday evening, with the help of some of the other men at the retreat, he had loaded it onto a trailer, taken it to a field and used the containers for target practice. His distributors were none too happy with him, but he knew that it was a radical step that he must take in light of what God had shown Him.

The next day was Super Bowl Sunday. Church in America on

Super Bowl Sunday can often serve as a base for last-minute Super Bowl party planning. That was anything but the case at Colonial Hills Church in 1994. When the men came home from the retreat on Saturday afternoon, wives all over the county felt the need to send out all-points bulletins on their husbands. The men who showed up at their homes, they said, were not the ones who left for a retreat on Friday. Their curiosity, along with the stories of what God had done on the retreat, brought expectation for Sunday morning church unlike anything I have ever experienced.

God did not disappoint on Super Bowl Sunday. The seats were packed long before time for the service to begin. The altars were full before the service even started. Our missionary speaker told many of the same stories he had told through the weekend with the men sounding exclamation points by thundering, "Whoomp!" This was how one of the African tribal groups had expressed their agreement with the gospel when it was brought to them. The service ran into the early afternoon, and no one seemed to notice. We certainly didn't want to go home and miss anything.

Around two in the afternoon, our pastor told us to go home and eat and rest. Our evening service would conclude the weekend. It started at six o'clock, but our pastor announced that the doors would open earlier in the afternoon for anyone who wanted to come and pray before the service. Shortly after four o'clock, the church auditorium was packed. The choir began to sing long before six, and no one could really tell when the service actually started.

Our guest missionary was late for the service that night. He had been late several times to various appointments during his time with us because of mechanical issues with his old van that doubled as his hotel room (at his insistence). Sometime during the evening service, our pastor announced, "We need to buy this man a van," and we took a special collection to buy him a better vehicle.

Remember that $500 that Loretta and I had just used to start our savings account? I felt like the Lord was prompting us to give it toward this missionary's van. Loretta followed my lead, and we were grateful to be able to bless this man that the Lord had used in such a tremendous way in our lives and in our church. He left in the next day or two in a nice new van. But God's work in our church wasn't finished yet. Not by a long shot.

During the months following Super Bowl Sunday, the altars were filled week after week with black garbage bags full of pornography, alcohol, drugs, tobacco, and other evidence of the strongholds in people's lives being broken. There were many occasions when the altars were so full during worship that we continued to sing, repeating choruses and then whole songs and then songs weren't even planned. A few times, this continued for so long that Preacher never even preached, but nobody seemed to mind how long the services went. This was truly a move of God.

***

The greatest corporate move of God I have ever seen took place on a Wednesday night during that season at Colonial Hills. Preacher passed along some news that he had received from one of the businessmen in our church. The owner of the building that housed the only abortion clinic in north Mississippi let it be known that he was willing to part ways with the abortion doctor at the end of his lease if he could find another tenant for the building. That building was just less than a half-mile from where our church would soon build its new campus. Preacher repeated what he had learned and encouraged anyone who owned a business or knew someone who owned a business to look into leasing that space. He said nothing else about the matter.

During one of the first few songs that night, a young lady made her way to the front and handed our pastor two rings. She stated that she wanted to give them toward removing the abortion clinic from the property. Word spread and—though no one ever asked for money—a spirit of giving swept across the Wednesday night crowd. People began to bring cash and write checks. Others began to give cars, land, and other personal property.

Still others began to "redeem" property. This was essentially giving something of greater value than what had been given by someone else in order that the property be returned to the original owner. We saw people give items of great sentimental value out of obedience to the Lord's direction, only to receive those items back with joy when someone else redeemed them. A few even gave those possessions again *after* they were redeemed.

Standing near the top of the choir loft, I began to struggle with the weight of giving. We had given our entire savings to help buy the missionary a new van, so we had little of value. Except our cars. And Loretta's wedding ring. Giving one of the cars made no sense as we were both working in different directions at the time (not that the Lord's direction needed to made sense, as we were learning). I wasn't going to ask her to give her ring, yet the compelling desire to give would not go away.

Moments later, Loretta motioned for me to meet her at the altar to pray. After we had spent some time in prayer together, right before we were about to return to our seats, I told her that she could give her ring if the Lord spoke that to her. She began to weep because He had been convicting her to give it. We went together to our pastor.

"Preacher," I began, "you can vouch for us. We don't need this ring to prove that we're married. We want to give it."

"Ms. Lo-retta," he responded in his slow Southern drawl as he hesitated and looked directly into her beautiful gray-blue eyes, "are you *sure*?"

She nodded and turned loose of the ring. Preacher didn't keep it long, though. Some friends of ours had been feeling conviction to give something of their own. They had saved $2,000 toward a down payment on a new home but felt the tugging of the Holy Spirit to give it. When they saw Loretta let go of her ring, they felt conviction that God was asking for their down payment. They stepped forward and redeemed her ring.

The twists and turns of the life of faith don't always work out quite like that, but one part of the equation is always true: God doesn't exist within human understanding. What had once been to us a ring bought on credit spent a short time as a paid-for ring as I learned about honoring God with our finances. It then became a gift to help put a stop to the evil down the street. Today, it is much more than a $2,000 treasure. It is a symbol of our love for one another, of our friends' obedience to the Lord, and of the One who is still our greatest treasure.

***

Our church entered into negotiations for the building that housed the abortion clinic soon afterward. The leaseholder rejected contracts that our church offered three different times. Our pastor held up the last offer, and anyone sitting anywhere near the pulpit could see red markings all over it. He informed us that we would not be making another offer. We prayed as a church that night that the Lord would intervene once again in this work that He had begun. He did.

Within a few days of our church's prayer, the owner of the building was notified that bankruptcy proceedings were in process against him. In turn, he notified the church that he would agree to the third contract just as it had been written. Shortly thereafter, we had a lease on the building.

The abortion doctor was arrested shortly afterward on a variety of charges both in Mississippi and Alabama. Colonial Hills Church marched from our church past the property where our new church building would soon stand to our newly leased building to hold a worship service and thank God for doing what only He could have done. The building was soon be renovated and for a time, used as Sunday school space for young married couples.

***

Luke 17:5-6

The apostles said to the Lord, "Increase our faith!" And the Lord said, "If you had faith like a grain of mustard seed, you could say to this mulberry tree, 'Be uprooted and planted in the sea,' and it would obey you."

6 DARKNESS

I had heard rumors of plots against me by at least one of the parents of the 1992 team, but I had more or less dismissed them as time by the spring of 1994. I had hoped that the passing of time would soothe wounds and bring perspective to what had otherwise been a remarkable season with many memories to treasure. I had heard through a mutual friend, though, that one lady had threatened to "get him, no matter how long it takes."

***

One of the manifestations of the work God was doing in our church was a group from our neighborhood that began to meet from house to house, eating together, sharing life together and praying for one another just like the church in the book of Acts. This group, I discovered, was meeting practically every night of the week. I longed for this deeper connection with others who were passionately pursuing the Lord in every aspect of their lives.

I discovered what was going on with this group quite by accident one Sunday morning as the choir was getting ready for the morning service. I overheard my friend Barry Wilson mention something that had happened in the group. I probed a little and by the end of that week, I was a regular.

This was a foreshadowing of the small groups ministry of our church, which we would launch within a couple of years. I see now what a life-changing conversation that little chat with Barry in the choir room ultimately would be. Then, though, we both shook our heads curiously at how the Lord had led me so quickly to connect with those who already had established friendships with one another. We would not have to wait long to discover why that group—and Barry, in particular—would intersect with my life at that specific time.

***

In January of 1994, Loretta and I rejoiced with the news that we were expecting another baby. In the months since our church had purchased the former abortion clinic building, an inordinate number of families in our church had lost babies to miscarriages. We had been one of them. At some point, someone recognized that this might be a spiritual attack, and our church prayed against what we believed to be attacks on the unborn. After that prayer, healthy babies became the norm again.

Our first child had been due in July. This child was to be born near the end of October. We began to discuss and pray about options for taking care of our baby. Though we knew it would mean surviving on a teacher's salary, we made the decision for

Loretta to leave her job with FedEx when our baby was born. That created quite a dilemma for us with another commitment we had made.

***

Our church had outgrown the campus just a block from our house in the Colonial Hills neighborhood of Southaven. We had agreed together to embark on the first of several three-word giving campaigns. The first—called Possess the Land—had been to purchase 17 acres on Highway 51. The second was dubbed Road to Glory, and its purpose was to pay for the massive building project on the new campus. (The third was Faith to Freedom, an attempt that fell short of its goal to pay off the debt that remained.)

Loretta and I had not felt much freedom to give before we finally broke through the barrier of the personal debt that we carried. Through our giving the $500 for the missionary's new van and giving Loretta's ring toward the shutting down of the abortion clinic, we were a quick study in God's ability to provide if we would just step out in faith to give when He led. We had received unexpected funds along the way, like the return of the apartment security deposit, on several occasions.

My favorite of God's provision was the time we received an income tax refund of $237 and did not have a pressing need for the money. While driving Ol' Bessie (our old baby blue Taurus, a story in God's provision in itself) to my parents' house, Loretta and I enjoyed discussing the various ways we could spend the money. Alas, the alternator in the car expired on the drive home, and our dog's leg was broken when a car hit him the following week. The grand total for a new alternator and care for Kirby was...$237.

Loretta and I made the choice not to see that income tax check as ours that we lost. Instead, we chose to thank God for supplying our need ahead of when we actually had them. That has been a repeated choice that has served us well through the years. The Road to Glory capital campaign would test our faith in God's ability to provide for our needs in a much larger way.

Over the course of several weeks, Loretta and I considered along with the rest of the church what we would give over the following three years. We prayed together about the amount. However, when the Lord began to reveal the amount to us individually, we could not bring ourselves to tell one another. Loretta thought that if she said the number the Lord had given her, I would laugh. I felt like she had no idea of the huge leap of faith involved in my number. Reaching an impasse, we decided to write our numbers down on scraps of paper, exchange them, and open them at the same time.

A moment on the verge of a great faith move contains a great deal of hope and excitement. Loretta and I allowed a pregnant pause before opening our individual pieces of paper. Slowly, we opened them to find that she had been right. I could not believe her number: $10,000. We were each making around $20,000 a year at that time, and we had a child on the way, Loretta's number seemed staggering. But her number was the same as mine.

***

We made our pledge and began to give. Just a year into our commitment, though, we reached a crisis of faith. We sensed that God was leading Loretta to stay home with our child, but we had divided out our commitment over three years. With Loretta's income we would be able to pay it off. Without her income we didn't even know if we would be able to scrape out a meager living, much less pay off such a sizable sum.

Why would the Lord lead us to make such a bold commitment that was a big enough stretch as it was and then call Loretta to stay home with our child? We answered that question by doing what He had told us last. We would continue to give until Loretta stepped away from her job to be at home full time. We would worry about the rest of our commitment then and trust that God would make a way for what He had called us to do.

***

In the midst of the excitement of everything the Lord was doing in our church and in our lives, spring brought another baseball season. I didn't know quite what to make of the collection of talent of the 1994 edition of the Hernando Tigers. That season appeared to be a transition year as a talented group of young players around whom I could build a competitive team gained experience. We were very inexperienced at some key positions, but sometimes young teams arrive a little earlier than expected. I had high hopes that this would be one of those teams.

After a few ups and downs early in the season, my team faced a very talented team from Tennessee in a high-caliber tournament up the road in Millington, Tennessee. Their pitcher made quick work of the top of our order in the first inning and looked for all the world like he had no-hitter type stuff that night. In the second inning, the game turned. My cleanup hitter led off the frame for us, quickly fell behind in the count, and then laced one of the hardest line drives I've ever seen back up the middle for a base hit. Like someone had flipped a switch, our offense, defense, and pitching looked as dominant in that game as any the 1992 team had played. In the remaining hour-and-a-half of that game, my expectations for the team soared.

Two days later, playing on a big stage in what was then the USA Olympic team's training complex, we lost 18-1. My shortstop made four errors that day, and the rest of the team didn't fare much better. We looked as bad that day as we had looked good two days earlier. That was a microcosm of the season for us. One day, the young talent seemed on the verge of breaking through for good. The next, as Coach Pierce used to say in my student coaching days, we "looked like Ned and the primer."

With about a week to go in the season, I received what seemed like a very odd visit from a parent. She came pointing her finger and accusing me of not caring about the parents of my players. After settling into a more rational conversation, this mother asked if there was anything she could do to help. This was not a lady who was around the team much; I don't even remember if I had even met her before that day. She was certainly not someone I knew well. I thanked her for her offer of assistance but told here that the school administration took care of gate receipts and that the Diamond Girls took care of concessions so that parents did not need to miss their sons' games. The mother seemed nice enough by that point, so I didn't think much more about it. Until a week or two later.

＊

On May 2, 1994, I was given notice that somehow a large group of parents had gained audience with the school board to air a laundry list of complaints against me. I was not made aware of these complaints, nor was my principal, nor was the school superintendent. Obviously, someone had been bending the ear of at least one of the school board members for this matter to come before them without following the proper chain of command.

An aging former lawyer brought the charges against me on behalf of "approximately 60 parents." For the board's convenience and so as not to crowd the meeting room, he said, he would be bringing the charges on their behalf (though he personally had nothing against me). Not a single parent attended the school board meeting that day. The veil between the charges and those who brought them, however, was extremely thin.

The headline in our local newspaper the next day read, "Parents Complain of Coach's Behavior." The article summarized the charges in the categories of "favoritism and religious harassment." I allegedly "verbally attacked and degraded players personally, in the classroom and on the field, about their appearance...and how they conduct themselves on a daily basis, both in and out of school."

I had plenty to say in response to most of these allegations. I mean, it wasn't out of the ordinary for a coach in any sport to "verbally abuse" a player by telling him to get a haircut or to "degrade players personally...in the classroom" by suspending players who skipped class. Most of the charges could be seen for what they were by rational minds. The most dangerous ones contained some truth, albeit twisted. Others were downright bizarre.

Instead of speaking about the list of allegations publicly at that board meeting or in the press, I decided to respond with the professionalism that I felt had not been extended to me. I painstakingly crafted my response in a letter to the school board, carefully answering each of the 17 often-redundant charges in my own letter to the board. I also offered to meet with the school board personally to respond to the allegations. My response turned into a coaching manifesto, of sorts, and served to solidify my coaching philosophy.

In the weeks that followed, as the baseball team completed my first losing season as a head coach, I received an outpouring of support from players, parents, students, and teachers. Many parents of current and former players let me know that they were certainly not represented by the statements to the school board. I knew that already, but I was encouraged by the expressions of confidence in my ability to run the Hernando baseball program.

***

My principal and I were indeed called before the board as they met in executive session a couple of weeks later. Unfortunately, my principal had a prior obligation that prevented his being in attendance. He did, however, write his own letter to the board expressing his unswerving support of me as a coach and teacher at his school.

With the lack verifiable evidence—not to mention the failure of any of the accusing parents to even sign their name to their complaints, much less appear in front of the board—I expected a quick meeting. I expected them to be able to see through the accusations to find a few bitter parents lashing out at their sons' coach. Instead, I learned a lesson in small town politics.

One of the board members stated that he was tired of hearing about what was going on in the Hernando baseball program. I did not know this particular board member, but I did know that he was friendly with one of the upset parents from the 1992 team. He—and the rest of the board—agreed that the charges were unsubstantiated, at best. Nevertheless, he made this statement: "My mama always told me that where there's smoke, there's bound to be at least a little bit of fire."

I was dumbfounded and had no response to his statement. When I related my experience to Loretta later that evening, her first question was, "Hasn't he ever heard of arson?" It was probably good that I had not thought to offer that suggestion.

Until that day, I had not even given a thought to my being anywhere but Hernando High School the following year. I still had the backing of my principal, other teachers, students, and parents. The day of the second board meeting, I began to consider that the Lord might have had other plans for me. I wondered if He was asking for my 40-years-at-one-school plan just four years into it.

***

After the meeting with the school board, I knew I had a decision to make. I didn't mind weathering the storm, and I appreciated the confidence that those in my school had given me. But something inside me had clicked. Instinctively, I felt like the time had come for me to leave. However, I did not want to make a decision of that magnitude without counsel.

My first visit after the school board meeting was to Bill Tharp's office. One of the pastors at my church at that time, he was a trusted adviser and friend. He listened as I laid out all the goings-on of the past two years and especially of the prior couple of weeks. He affirmed my thoughts that the process was not as it should have been and agreed that a case might even be made for slander. Then, he asked a game-changing question.

"Al, what do you feel like the Lord is telling you to do?"

"It Is Well (with My Soul)," I answered, naming the popular old hymn.

Every time I had prayed about my situation since the allegations first arose, I felt a great sense of peace and of God's control as I prayed. Much of my praying was done while walking the streets of my neighborhood. There were many times that I began singing "It Is Well" aloud as I walked and prayed and sensed God's presence there with me.

When Bill asked me what God was telling me, I knew what I should do. I released control of the situation. I would allow the Lord to do with it what He pleased. If the time had indeed come to move on, I would do so graciously. If not, I would stay and do my job with greater resolve. Somehow, though, I still sensed that I would soon be moving in a new direction further away from my career plan.

***

In addition to our small group meetings that were still going on more nights than not, I spent quite a few afternoons after school in conversation with Barry Wilson. The days seemed longer than ever. In addition to the spring fever that hits high school students after spring break and makes keeping their concentration increasingly difficult as the school year plays out, I was being pressed by each passing day to make a decision about my future. Barry became my sounding board.

Barry was the one who first told me about the small group that I had now been attending for several months whenever my schedule would allow. He was the one who had wondered aloud why the Lord led me that direction. He was also the one who was going through a similar decision-making process about his own job. We came to understand why the Lord had thrust us together as we talked and prayed together.

Many aspects of my decision caused me to waver. My principal had insisted that I would have a job at Hernando as long as I wanted it; however, he needed to be able to have as much time as he could to hire a new coach, should it come to that. As good as he had been to me, I certainly wanted to afford him as much time as possible. A dear family in our school had suggested a conversation with the principal at Southern Baptist Educational Center, where their children had been enrolled prior to coming to Hernando.

SBEC was looking for a new baseball coach, and the timing seemed appropriate to my situation. Just up the road in Southaven, this was Loretta's high school alma mater, so I had some ties to the school through her. I was not going to make a decision strictly based on circumstances, but I did have to pay attention to them.

***

When the relationships among players and parents had broken down in 1992, I had spared Loretta many of the details. We were not yet married then, so I had tried to protect her as much as possible from some of the backlash. Now, she was feeling it full force. We had scheduled her last day at FedEx before coming home to be with our child for the beginning of May. My leaving Hernando High School without accepting another job first would have meant zero income for our soon-to-be family of three.

I began conversations with the principal at SBEC during that last month of school, but it became apparent that no job offer was forthcoming quickly. I felt encouraged by our conversations, but they, too, were trying to complete a school year. I stuck to the task of finishing out my own commitments in the classroom and soon found myself preparing for semester exams with no resolution to my career path in sight.

***

I was giving my first period exam when Mrs. Ward came to my door to tell me that my wife was on the phone and needed to talk to me. An eerie feeling swept immediately over me. Just a semester earlier, this was the exam I had been giving when she had called about fears of losing our first child. I moved quickly toward the phone in the school office, where my fears were confirmed. She was bleeding and needed me to take her to the doctor.

Mrs. Ward again spoke words of peace and encouragement over me as she took my place in giving my exams. As I made the twenty-minute drive home, I pleaded with the Lord to give me whatever it would take to lead my wife through this again. I had felt so helpless before, and He had given us both what we needed to make it through. To have if happen again so quickly might be more than Loretta could take. I expected her to already be coming apart at the seams.

When I arrived home, I found Loretta scared but in control. While I had been rushing home, she had been praying. The Lord had given her a peace that she would be okay. We moved quickly to get her to the doctor to see if the same would be true for our baby. With everything playing out so hauntingly similar to the same experience just five months earlier, we prepared for the worst.

As we waited for the ultrasound technician, I considered how differently the grieving period might be this time. With all the Lord had done in our church, with all the families we now knew who had gone through miscarriage, with our own experience—it would be better this time, I hoped and prayed. Loretta and I kept a brave front for one another, but inside we both expected the worst. We did not at all expect the technologist's words, spoken in a singsong manner: "I see a healthy little heartbeat."

There are times when the priorities in life that should rise to the top actually do rise unmistakably to the top. This was one of those days. My wife was okay. Our baby was alive and healthy and still progressing toward a late-October birthday. Decisions about my professional future and our financial commitment to our church could wait. This was a good day.

The Lord called on Loretta and me to trust Him in many ways that didn't make much sense outside of His leading in the early years of our marriage. When we wouldn't see what was around the corner, He reassured us that He was, indeed, in control. Our faith grew exponentially as our spiritual eyes adjusted to the darkness that always accompanies a life of faith.

***

Hebrews 11:6

And without faith it is impossible to please him, for whoever would draw near to God must believe that he exists and that he rewards those who seek him.

7 UPSIDE DOWN

I had a problem saying no. I wanted to prove myself capable and excel at my job. Any new opportunity that arose, I took it. I even volunteered for some additional responsibilities. Every one of those decisions seemed altruistic at the time. But I was becoming a stranger in my own home.

***

By the fall of 1994, I had started a new job as an English teacher and coach of high school baseball, junior high football, and junior high basketball at Southern Baptist Educational Center (now Northpoint Christian School). Conversations with SBEC had lasted well into the summer. When I felt like the talks with SBEC were progressing toward a position there, I freed Mr. Long at Hernando from any obligation he felt like he owed to hold my position open. He had found a young coach that he wanted to hire but promised me a teaching position if I chose to return.

I was accustomed to teaching a full schedule of classes and coaching high school baseball, but I would now be adding junior high football and basketball coaching duties to my plate. Aside from the year at Charleston—where I coached football receivers and defensive backs for a single season—I didn't bring any experience with those sports to my new position. I learned on the job through others on the coaching staff.

***

On October 26, 1994—just two months into my new job—Loretta and I welcomed Ashton Leigh Ainsworth into the world. She was a great baby and grew into the cutest little two-year-old that the world has ever known. She loved to sing and play and dance. And when she smiled, everyone smiled with her.

My new responsibilities, some of which I had voluntarily added to an already-full slate, kept me away from home far too much. Often, as she grew older, Ashton would carry a photo of me with her. When she would meet someone new, she would point to the photo and say, "This is my daddy."

I would leave for work every day before Ashton awakened. Many nights, she would already be asleep when I returned home. She was too young to know anything was out of the ordinary, but Loretta was feeling the loneliness of being a coach's wife. I coached alongside two other guys about my age. Each of us carried a full class schedule, coached three sports, and felt the weight of our schedules.

We did, however, have an advocate. Our athletic director, Coach Jim Philpot, had been coaching for decades and had been where we were. He had seen the toll that schedules like ours took on families. He told the upper administration repeatedly that if they didn't lighten our load, they would burn us out. He once asked each of the sport coaches to give up a percentage of our budgets so that the school could hire another coach. We agreed, excited about getting some help and some relief. Much to all of our chagrin, though, the additional coach was not added to our staff, and the money was never returned to our budgets.

During my second year at SBEC, I learned that my personal schedule was about to become more crowded. Loretta and I were expecting a second child, a son who would arrive during the football season of 1996. Even with the welcomed relief in my school schedule, some tough decisions awaited me as the leader of my family.

***

A couple of weeks before Ashton's second birthday, we took her to Chuck E. Cheese (where a kid can be a kid, as the jingle goes) as her last outing as a single child. Our son was due in a few weeks, and we wanted to celebrate one last time as a family of three. As it turned out, that night was to be our last opportunity.

Our friends David and Debbie Martin had welcomed their second daughter, Samantha, to the world that day, so after hanging out with Chuck E. and the gang for a while and eating our fill of pizza, we stopped by the hospital to pay them a quick visit. Loretta made herself comfortable on the floor as we chatted with the Martins until visiting hours were over. As I reached down to help Loretta up, her eyes met mine, and she gave a quick shake of her head.

"You're not about to have that baby now, are you?" I joked.

"Umm. Think so," she responded with a grimace.

We were already in the right hospital, so we went downstairs so that they could have a look. Sure enough, she was ready to deliver. After some scrambling to secure a babysitter for Ashton until my in-laws could rush back into town to take care of her, I returned to the hospital with the appropriate bags. Birth was not imminent, so we settled in for a long night.

Garrett Allen Ainsworth made his appearance the next morning. He was born a few weeks early and had to spend his first few nights in the Neonatal Intensive Care Unit. His lungs had not fully developed, and he eventually went home on an apnea monitor. Loretta became especially adept at carrying his car seat and accompanying equipment everywhere she went over the next four months.

Garrett's first name was my grandmother's middle name. The *Allen*, though, is the name around which a special legacy is being built in our family. Garrett is the fourth generation *Allen*. No juniors. My full name is Allen Wade, my dad's name is Luther Allen, and his father's name was Thomas Allen. I'm hoping to be alive to see another generation or two of this legacy unfold.

Other than for battery issues, the apnea monitor did not register any problems in the four months that we lugged it around. (And by *we*, I mean mainly Loretta.) The night after Garrett came off the monitor, though, he awoke with severe breathing problems. A severe case of croup was eventually diagnosed as the culprit. An ambulance ride and several breathing treatments later, we returned home exhausted. This was the first of several croup episodes with Garrett, but with each one, we (meaning mainly Loretta) learned to care for our growing little family.

***

With two children at home to care for now, Loretta tried desperately to get me to see how much she needed me home more, not to mention how much my kids needed me there. I was resistant, though, rationalizing that my position as a coach was more important than my role at home. After all, I was responsible for more kids there. And it was, after all, a Christian school, and I needed to be there providing them a solid foundation for life.

I was feeling pressure, for sure, but my heart was still torn between my family—whom I loved—and my job, which I also loved. I can be a slow learner at times. Loretta exhausted her means of helping me see and began to turn over my misplaced priorities to the Lord. Ever so slowly, I began to hear from Him and make some changes.

***

One summer, as soon as baseball season was over, I looked forward to relaxing by playing some church softball as I had every summer since I moved to the area. That, as it turned out, was the proverbial straw that broke the camel's back. Softball was normally scheduled for one, maybe two nights per week. One week still pretty early in the season, though, a stretch of make-up games caused a week filled with softball. Loretta was not happy. I had to make a choice.

I made a sort of backhanded comment during one of our period of intense fellowship regarding my priorities. "What do you want me to do, quit playing softball?" I asked.

Yes, came the answer. Yes. Quit playing softball.

So I did. But not with the attitude of a husband who suddenly "got it." My eyes were only slightly more open than they were when I had gone out of town on a basketball trip (with the varsity team, with whom I had no official responsibilities). When I arrived home, Loretta wasn't home, so I rode with the varsity coach to scout another game. Yeah, bad move.

Slowly, over the course of the summer, I began to notice that if I was at home with my family, I didn't even think about the softball games that I was missing. That was the way my thought pattern worked. I didn't think about where I wasn't; I fully engaged with where I was. I just wasn't choosing to be in the place

83

that mattered most—home—often enough. But that was beginning to change.

***

Several years later, I would recognize that the transformation toward my embracing the choice to place my priorities at home was complete. I remember standing in the third base coach's box at Horn Lake High School. My team was on the verge of falling by the mercy rule without managing so much as a hit. Earlier in my career, I would have been livid with my team's lack of effort and very possibly used the extra daylight for some extra "conditioning" work for my team.

On this day, however, my thoughts went something more like this: "Wow, this game's barely an hour old. If they hold us here and score a run, I can get home in time to do a little work in the garden." I wasn't giving up as a coach, but when you've been around baseball for a while, you recognize that sometimes, that day just isn't your day. That was one of those days. There would be some unexpected time at the end of the daylight hours, and I planned to make the most of it. At home.

***

Not long after Garrett was born, I was out walking alone in the neighborhood and doing some praying. I had begun to notice that our back yard was feeling smaller and smaller the more active Ashton became. As I was walking and praying, I told the Lord that if He wanted us to stay in our little house with our little yard, I would choose to be content. If, however, I "had not because I had asked not," well, I was asking. I grew up in the country where there was room to run and play outside, and I wanted my children to be able to enjoy that, too.

Loretta and I had discussed building a house, but it seemed out of the realm of possibility. Though we might have been able to afford to build the house, there was that pesky part of the plan where we would have to buy a plot of land on which to build it. I

84

expected the Lord to reveal a way to afford a house with a bigger yard or to settle my soul back into contentment. He did not answer my prayer in either fashion, instead reminding me of a commitment we had made to Him several years before.

The three-year giving campaign at church to which we had committed $10,000 had ended, and another was set to begin. We had stopped giving with over $6,000 still remaining on our pledge when Loretta had come home to care for our children. God reminded me on my prayer walk that our commitment had not been so much to the church but to Him. But, Lord, I argued, do you know how much I make and how close we are cutting it already? Yes, as it turned out, He did know.

Loretta and I resolved to take a step of faith, carving our family budget deeply to eke out $25 per month to give toward our pledge. At that rate we would complete our commitment in a little over 20 years. However, we were now, by faith, dealing with God's economy.

With the side money I made throwing newspapers with my friend Bill—in addition to our $25 per month throughout the year—we completed our commitment within two years. During that time we also upgraded our family car from baby blue Ol' Bessie to a more dependable car whose air conditioner was actually functional.

I don't remember exactly how much time passed before we joyfully completed our promise—a few weeks at most—until we received a phone call that both changed the course of our family and sent our faith through the roof. Unbeknownst to us, Loretta's parents had been looking at neighborhood lots on our behalf and had found one they thought would be a good one for us. And they wanted to buy it for us. I felt like I was living the story of Jesus' feeding the five thousand. Our $25 per month was about to multiply into a bigger house with a bigger yard for our family to be able to run and play and enjoy.

***

We lived with my in-laws while we were building our new house, and we moved it Thanksgiving weekend of 1998. We were leaving behind a large neighborhood of small houses stacked on one another. Most of those houses had been built in the 1960's with one-car carports, most of which had long since been taken in to add housing space. As a result, cars lined the streets on either side, giving the neighborhood an even more crowded feel.

In these little houses, though, we had enjoyed some of the most authentic and intimate times of Acts 2-type fellowship with other Christ-followers that we have ever known. We ate meals together, prayed together, played together, served our community together, and so much more. I even learned to swim as a 35-year-old adult from Gary, a guy in my group that I trusted, even in the water. Some of this "doing life together" came before small groups was ever an official ministry of our church. It continued after our church made the transition from Sunday school to small groups as the primary discipleship arm of ministry.

I think that the less pretense people have about knowing how to lead a ministry, the more comfortable people feel about muddling through that ministry together. Compared to today, we had no idea what we were doing back then. But we genuinely loved the Lord and believed that He could do anything, so spending time with the precious few other people in our lives who lived that way just felt rather intuitive. Week after week, the little bands of believers in our neighborhoods saw God do what only He could do.

One particular instance stands above all the others. We were meeting at Tommy and Michele Henley's house in the Brook Hollow neighborhood near Southaven High School. The house where they lived back then might have been about 900 square feet, and we crammed a dozen or more adults in there, plus about a half-dozen kids. Loretta's heart was heavy as she brought a prayer need to group that would require the Lord's intervention.

Problems with her eyes had sent Loretta to our ophthalmologist, a friend of ours from church and the man from whom we had bought our first little house. He was very concerned with what he saw and was fearful of where it might lead. Loretta informed our group of what she knew at that time, and we began to pray earnestly on her behalf.

God was answering many of our prayers during that season. I don't try to undertake the fruitless task of trying to figure God out, so I don't know why we saw so many answers to prayer during that time. We didn't have some secret prayer formula, but our hearts were genuinely seeking Him. We didn't believe there was anything He couldn't do.

One of the most memorable aspects of what the Lord was doing in our group during that season of life together was how His answers intermingled in many of our prayers. This happened on the night that we prayed for Loretta's eyes. I had been praying that God would teach me to know when I had heard from Him about big faith moves. As we prayed for Loretta's eyesight that night, I heard a voice in my head so clear that it might as well have been audible, saying simply, "It's done." I opened my eyes, expecting everyone else to have been similarly impressed. They continued to pray. I responded by lowering my head, closing my eyes, and re-joining them in prayer.

"I said it's done. Are you going to believe Me?" God was putting me to the test even as He answered my ongoing prayer to hear from Him. It was a pivotal moment of faith for me. I could wait to see if He would truly answer our prayer, or I could speak aloud what I was convinced He had already spoken to me.

"It's done," I said weakly. Though Loretta felt no sudden physical change, we celebrated as if our prayer had been answered. We believed that it had. A visit to the doctor the following week confirmed an answered prayer. Dr. Smith told Loretta that he had not wanted to scare her prematurely but that her condition would likely have led to blindness at a young age. With our having two very young children, that news would have been devastating. His follow-up exam showed none of the evidence that had been there before.

"I believe you've seen a miracle," he said.

***

I would be remiss to write about the small group meeting where my wife's eyes were miraculously healed and leave out my single favorite small group moment in over 20 years of meeting with other believers in small groups. The group had an extended time of prayer that night. By the time it was over, we were all lying prostrate on the floor in the Henleys' tiny den. I don't remember who was keeping watch over our toddlers in a room in the back of the house, but before we had said the last *amen*, the kids were turned loose to go back to their parents.

Usually, after what was typically a two-hour small group meeting, the kids came back in with two hours' worth of pent-up energy to tell us what they had learned and to show us the pictures they had colored or the crafts they had made. On this night, though, they crept into the den so silently during our prayer that we were hardly aware of them. We couldn't help but notice them after our prayers were exhausted. Lifting our eyes, we saw a layer of children spread on top of their praying parents, soaking it all in and imitating what they were seeing.

I remember standing in the kitchen later that night with Denny Burt, our small group leader. We knew that what we had just seen had significance that would not be quickly lost on anyone who had seen it. He voiced what he and I were both thinking, that if we could fumble around and figure out this small group thing even just a little bit, how much further would they be able to go in their faith journeys?

Of all the remarkable experiences of the season of the mid-1990's in our church, this picture of children building on their parents' faith foundation continues to be the most pertinent to me. In light of what God has led me to do now—to help others pass their values from one generation to the next through the stories they tell...and re-tell—I believe the fervent prayers from the Henleys' living room on a night long ago continue to be answered today.

***

Hebrews 12:28-29

Therefore let us be grateful for receiving a kingdom that cannot be shaken, and thus let us offer to God acceptable worship, with reverence and awe, for our God is a consuming fire.

A note on this Scripture: Years ago, God taught me a simple but profound way to pray: Acknowledge that he is a consuming fire. Recognize that anything that is consumed is gone and not to be recovered. Then, confess that He is worthy of anything He chooses to consume. Finally, be amazed that what He can produce is infinitely more valuable that what I allowed Him to pry from my fingers in the first place.

8 WHITE KNUCKLES

I've never wanted so badly NOT to take the high road. I wanted to lash out at my accusers, and I had plenty of players and parents who would have backed me if I had done so. I had taken responsibility for my part of the debacle, but our team was still held captive by accusation. We would all learn a valuable lesson in restraint, perseverance, and submission to our authorities that season.

***

Our little family of four moved out of the little house on Ashland Drive to live with Loretta's parents while we built our new house on our new, paid-for two-acre lot. Not until Loretta's dad knocked down the head-high weeds with his tractor and mowing deck did we know what the land actually looked like. It was beautiful. Trees lined both sides, and the house site sat on a little hill. There was a sharp rise in the backyard toward the bean fields to which it backed up, but we could move much of that dirt around front to help with drainage issues.

Some old friends of ours had once told us that if we would build a new house every two years, then we could be living in our dream home by the third house. They even volunteered to help us do it. The strategy seemed risky to me, but they seemed to be having success with it. I don't know that we could have stomached moving that many times, but here we were, ready to try it once, anyway.

We had fallen out of touch with William and Shari but reached out to them with a couple of questions as we began the building process. Shari was a contractor and knew the ropes. A few minutes into Loretta's conversation with her, she reminded us that she still wanted to help us build a house and volunteered her and William's time and expertise.

I thought back to the prayer walk I had taken through the Colonial Hills neighborhood. What the Lord required of us—the paying off of the remaining $6,000 of our pledge to the church—had seemed so far beyond our means that we could never hope to build a house. Now, just a couple of years later, we were ready to start building a house. It seemed surreal.

I had earned over $6,000 above and beyond the expenses we needed to live during that time. We had paid off all of our debt and profited $20,000 on the sale of our house just five years after we bought it. We were living rent-free with Loretta's folks, who had given us a two-acre lot to build a larger house on a lot with plenty of room for the kids to play. Our friends were contracting the house for us at no charge. We were serving as cleanup crew, painters, and landscapers. To top it all off, my mom financed the house for us at a lower interest rate than we could have gotten through a bank.

When all was said and done, we moved into a much larger house on a much larger lot and paid the same mortgage payment as before...and for eight fewer years. I had scraped out $25 per month as a step of faith that the Lord would help us do what we had committed Him to do. The Lord responded to a short prayer and a $25 step of faith with tens of thousands of dollars in return, not to mention a faith that was expanded beyond what I could have even comprehended. It was an increased faith that I would need within just a few years.

***

Life was plenty busy for our little family in the mid- to late-90's. I was still learning to turn my heart toward home, where Ashton and Garrett were growing up quickly. Though the Lord was changing my heart and my priorities, my teaching and coaching job still required many hours. I was still very passionate about building a viable program at a school that was not known for baseball. Coach Philpot had won us young coaches an extra planning period and a season off from coaching by this time, a win never documented in any record book but one that made a huge difference in my home.

Regretfully, my friend Marty left SBEC for another job in Georgia. That broke up our self-proclaimed Lunch Bunch of Brenda Case, Thomas Vanderslice, Marty, and me. Brenda coached ninth-grade girls basketball, and Thomas was a long-time coach who now worked in the office of the church on whose campus the school was located. Along with our daily lunch that we ate in Marty's office, we shared our victories and losses from the fields and courts and classrooms. It was a safe place to learn from each other, to air out grievances, and to hold each other in account for any attitudes that were less than Christ-like. It was, I suppose, a second small group for me.

***

The baseball program's growth was slow but steady. Our record usually hovered around the .500 mark, but we played increasingly strong competition. When I arrived at SBEC, the most talented group in the school's history was the sophomore class. Unfortunately for the baseball program, though, those players are best remembered for their exploits on the football field and basketball court. Only one played baseball as a senior. As a result, we built the program around a group of younger players.

The players from a large freshman class from my first year at the school would ultimately leave their mark on the program as a group who did their best to respect the game by the effort they gave it. Future classes would not have to be taught this respect as it was passed down from one class to the next. One of the greatest senses of accomplishment I felt from my years at SBEC was in watching one generation of players unselfishly teach the next the skills and the attitude that was giving our teams increasing success on the field. We would all later discover that—just like a reputation—what is built over many years could be torn down much more quickly.

When that initial freshman class of players had graduated, I received an infusion of talent unlike any I had ever experienced. A group of four players from various public schools in our county enrolled at our private Christian school and tried out for the team. They had tried out and been cut from their respective public school teams, but I felt like they could help us immediately. Within two years, they were realizing their potential on our team as we competed with the top public and private school teams in any classification in our area.

SBEC had competed in the Mississippi Private School Association (MPSA) since moving from Memphis to Southaven, Mississippi, in the 1980's. As enrollment grew, so did our classification until we were competing at the highest level of MPSA competition. This also meant drives of over three hours to play most district opponents and an hour-and-a-half to play our nearest district rival. The travel for all of our teams was an enormous drain on our athletic budget, so our administration looked into other options and found a very viable one.

The school was originally incorporated in Tennessee and still held that original charter. As a result of that technicality, the school applied for and was granted admission to the Tennessee Secondary Schools Athletic Association (TSSAA). This was enormously important on a couple of different levels. First, we would travel about an hour to our most distant district opponent; all the rest were within 30 minutes of our campus. Second, our pool of non-district competition increased dramatically.

***

The National Federation of High Schools is the national governing board for high school extra-curricular competition, including athletics. The National Federation recognizes only one governing body from each state. In Tennessee the TSSAA governed both public and private schools. There were separate public and private school championships, but they all played under the same set of guidelines. Mississippi's high school athletic governing body, as recognized by the National Federation, is the Mississippi High School Activities Association (MHSAA). The National Federation did not recognize the MPSA, under whose authority we had formerly played.

As a new member of a reciprocating state association, SBEC was now free to play Mississippi public schools. Before, this was impossible without specifically granted permission from both the MPSA and MHSAA. I immediately added to our schedule the public schools in our area whose coaches were willing to play us. I felt like our program, especially with its latest infusion of talent, could compete with any school of any size in our area.

We held our own against public school teams from Mississippi, notching wins over several area playoff-caliber teams.

95

Our small private school division schedule was less compelling, and we swept through that competition with little struggle, recording perfect district records for our first few years in TSSAA. At that time in TSSAA, all private schools—regardless of size—competed against one another for one state championship. The deck was certainly stacked against us in this regard. A run of *Hoosiers* magnitude would have been required for a small school to win a state title as the baseball playoffs were then configured. We played tough games with the larger schools and even won an occasional game against them, but we annually bowed out to the bigger schools in the regional tournament.

Having competed well with the larger private schools in our division and having an abundance of returning talent over the next two years, I liked our school's chances of being the first small school to advance past the district level of the state tournament. We would not have a chance to find out, however. The four public school newcomers, having gained traction in our program, all departed for those same public schools that had rejected them two years earlier. In addition, two more of our talented and experienced young players took their talents to the county public schools.

This was quite a blow to our program. With our school and the transfer schools all being National Federation members, my understanding was that the players should have to sit out a year unless their families actually moved, which they had not. If they had come to our school from a public school in our district after they had entered ninth grade, that would have been the case. The MHSAA viewed the transfers as if we had still been members of the MPSA. The salt in the wound, then, was that not only had we lost six good young baseball players but also that our freedom to play the local schools had served to showcase how talented those players were to the very schools that would lure them away.

The bad news for our baseball program was that most of our experience was now gone. The good news was that another class of very talented players would be entering ninth grade, and we would be able to build back around them. Most of these student-athletes had attended SBEC since kindergarten and were much more likely to stay through the end of their high school careers. These were players that I had taught in the classroom; I had coached some of them in junior high basketball. They were my kind of players—gritty, unselfish gamers. I was hesitant to move forward, however.

***

I had built a successful baseball program and won a junior high basketball championship at a school where the pressure to win was not intense. I felt like I was coming into my own as an English and social studies teacher, improving each year. However, I could also hear that small but persistent voice of the Lord trying to get my attention. I did not want to hear what He had to say.

My priorities were getting straightened out with home and work. My job performance evaluations were always beyond satisfactory. I was growing in the coaching profession, earning respect from many of the larger schools in our area for guiding our program to the success that it enjoyed. Even with the recent defections, our program was still on the upswing. Our facilities had improved every year, and we had even sent a few players to play at the collegiate level. But the Lord seemed to be asking for my job.

I remember the night it came to a head. I was at my best friend's house, where I unloaded everything that was going on and what the Lord seemed to be asking of me, what He was asking of the guy with the 40-years-at-the-same-school plan that He had already adjusted twice. During the course of our conversation, I wondered aloud what I would do, what I *could* do if I no longer taught and coached. "What else couldn't you do?" my friend responded.

I had never considered any career beyond what I had trained and called to do. Sure, I had the ability to teach and coach and train others in a variety of settings, but I had always boxed those skills into a high school setting. My friend's question caused me to consider that the Lord had something in mind for me that was, perhaps, outside of that box. We hit the floor in prayer, and the struggle was on. I did not release my dreams, goals, and career expectations easily. After a long period of wrestling back and forth with the Lord through tears, I gave in.

Ultimately, I had to confess that I had made God the boss of my life and—as the boss—he had the right to do with my life what best suited His purposes. When we closed our session of prayer that night, I was relieved in a way, happy to have released this burden and looking forward—albeit with much trepidation—to what He had next for me.

Then, the Lord who had wrestled my career from my grasp did something peculiar. He gave it back. As sure as I felt the reluctant release of my life as a baseball coach to God, I was just as sure of its return. I can't really explain what that looked or felt like, but I was prepared to take on the next school year, in general, and baseball season, in particular, with vigor and purpose at a whole new level. I had endured what seemed like double roller coaster loops—my life turning upside down, back level, upside down again, and back level again—and was now speeding toward...whatever was next.

***

I reached a unique marker in my life during that period of time. I received a phone call from a friend of mine from church. Kevin Newton wanted to know if I would help fill in for some players who couldn't make it to their church softball team's game one night. I had not played softball in a couple of years and honestly did not miss it. I was reluctant to even ask Loretta's opinion, but she said to go and play. She asserted that she knew my heart was at home and that one softball game couldn't hurt. Knowing my obsessive personality perhaps better than she did, I wasn't so sure.

I played that game and a couple more to close out the season for that team. I was saying my goodbyes to my temporary teammates after our final league game when Kevin asked if I wanted to go to Jackson to play in the state tournament. I had played in the Baptist state softball tournament every summer when I had played regularly. It was always a good chance to play one last tournament to close out the season, to visit some with my parents who lived nearby, and to rekindle old friendships with acquaintances from other parts of the state.

I had no desire to play in any more softball state tournaments at that point in my life, though. In the past we had regularly lost on Friday night and been eliminated early on Saturday after a game or two. I politely but determinedly declined Kevin's invitation. As I was walking away from Kevin to go to my car and say goodbye to softball forever, he grinned a sneaky grin that he possesses and said, "Richie's going to be there."

Richie Corder had been my best friend and my roommate before Loretta and I were married. He had moved away, and I rarely saw or talked to him. Still single because of that pesky requirement he has jokingly maintained that any potential bride for him still have all of her teeth, Richie is one of the most fun people I have ever been around. I ran it past Loretta, and she said, "Go." I went, and the Lord used softball as a vehicle for His work in and through my life for much of the next decade.

**

In the fall of 2000, I had another experience that I considered transformative even as it was happening. Even so, I had no idea just how the Lord would use one dramatic moment many times in the years to come. The setting was Team Trek, a team building camp with a high ropes course near Heber Springs, Arkansas. The administrators at SBEC had determined that a leadership retreat would be formative for each freshman class's high school careers. I went as a chaperone for the first of these retreats. At least that's why I thought I was going at the time.

One of the other male chaperones for the trip was Earl Williams, the father of one of my students. I confided in him that I was scared to death of heights. He had experienced Team Trek a number of times with his children and gave me a hint of what was to come. I could tell by the way he phrased certain responses, though, that he expected me to complete the obstacles along with the students in my group. Our Team Trek facilitator spoke to me much like Earl did. To lean upon a patently Southern phrase, I "broke nervous."

***

I was just about to begin my third year of teaching a class called Personal Enrichment for seventh grade boys. When I took over the class, the curriculum was more than a little outdated and largely irrelevant. I asked for and received permission to teach a curriculum based on Robert Lewis's excellent book *Raising a Modern-Day Knight*. The young men in this freshman class were the first that I had taught the principles of a real man:

A real man rejects passivity.

A real man takes responsibility.

A real man leads courageously.

A real man expects the greater reward (God's reward).

This group of young men had learned and embraced the principles wholeheartedly. They were about to discover that the man who had mentored them in the principles of manhood was a chicken, a fraud.

***

My team's first obstacle was called the Leap of Faith. It began with a series of railroad spikes extruding from a very large tree that led to a platform about 30 feet high. The object of the exercise was to climb the tree, walk to the edge of the platform, position one's toes just over the edge, and then leap toward a trapeze-looking bar about six to eight feet away. As if the platform weren't high enough, it stood at the edge of a gorge that made it appear much higher than it actually was.

Of course, every precaution was taken to properly harness and secure each participant. Whether a student (or teacher) grabbed the bar or missed it, a series of ropes secured to his harness made sure that he returned to the ground slowly and safely. I knew that the chances of getting hurt on this apparatus were remote. My brain knew that but forgot to communicate with my knees. They were wobbly as I stayed near the back of the pack, hoping that the time allotted for the exercise would expire before all eyes turned to me to see what I was going to do.

Several of the guys in my group volunteered immediately. Freshman boys, what did they know about precaution? Some climbed to the platform, walked determinedly across it, and fearlessly leaped for the swing. Jonathan Walker even pulled himself up on the bar and curled his legs around it to swing upside down for a few moments before floating to the ground. Some of the guys were nervous but followed through, and I could tell that they were both relieved to have done it and stimulated by the experience. I was enjoying watching their reactions until the line began to thin.

I looked repeatedly at my watch, hoping that the increased hesitation by those in the back of the line would eat up what was then plenty of time remaining. With just two or three participants left to go, Patrick Houston eased over beside me and asked, "You gonna do it, Coach?"

"I dunno, Patrick," I answered. I gave a flippant answer about making sure all the students had time for their turns. Patrick was a bigger guy who struggled academically. He was at least a year older than the other ninth graders, including his younger brother. Here, though, Patrick was in his element. Even at his young age, he had already experienced skydiving and racing sprint cars.

I'll never forget Patrick's approach to challenging me to take the "leap of faith." He didn't prod or tease. Instead, he reassuringly said, "You can do this." I could tell that somehow he knew that I wanted—no, needed—to do this. When somebody believes in me like that, I do not want to disappoint him. I determined to take my turn as soon as the last student's turn was over and before anyone else knew what a chicken I was.

My resolve diminished quickly when the final student participant froze halfway across the platform. Even with a tremendous round of encouragement from everyone standing below, he sat down and couldn't move for what must have been 10 minutes or more. Our time was slipping away quickly.

That was my out! I could walk away from the Leap of Faith having determined to jump without actually having the opportunity to jump. As the young man slowly reversed his steps and retreated down the tree, my brain forgot to communicate this concept with my heart. My heart knew that if I walked away from this challenge, I could not claim even a moral victory over my fears.

Our facilitator almost gathered everyone together and moved on to the next obstacle, but someone ratted me out. Well, they probably just asked me if I was going to go, but I was nevertheless exposed. All eyes were on me. All the eyes of these young men that I had taught to live up to the title of *young men*. I could not, would not let them down. I stepped forward with steely grit on the outside and maybe even just a little on the inside.

My determination was still intact as I ascended the spikes toward the platform (Don't look down, don't look down...). It remained strong until I reached about the halfway point of the opposite edge of the platform, right about where the guy before me had frozen. My strides shortened until I reached the last foot or so before the edge. Then, I inched slowly toward the leaping position, no longer daring to lose contact with the boards beneath me, even to take a small step. Finally, toes dangling over the edge, I was in leaping position.

I thought, what on earth have I done? There is no way.... Then, just as suddenly as that voice tried to talk me back, another one told me to just jump. Just. Jump. Don't think about it too long, or you won't do it at all, the voice said. Just count to three and jump. One. Two. Three!

I bent my knees and leaped from the platform. I remember my time in the air in slow motion. But not a fearful slow motion. No, somewhere between the time my feet left the Leap of Faith platform and the time my fingers securely wrapped around the bar of the swing, something clicked inside of me. As the group below me burst into applause, I knew that I would never be the same. I was right.

During the rest of the weekend, I climbed a rock wall and did a trust fall and zip lined across a cavernous gorge with very little fear. I watched with pride and great joy as the freshman class overcame the last obstacle as one big team. In talking with the other teachers and chaperones, though, I learned that they did or did not do the various obstacles by their own choice with no pressure from team leaders and facilitators. I'm glad I didn't feel like I had much of a choice but to participate. Someone knew that I would need the Leap of Faith exercise to prepare for what the following years of my life would hold.

***

After the Lord asked for my job and then returned it to me, I felt like I was back on track with my career goal but with even higher goals and purposes. With a practically brand-new group of players, my assistant coach and I went about laying a solid foundation of strong work ethic, teamwork, and good fundamentals. We took our lumps in the spring of 2001, but we had a strong core from which we expected success over the following years.

The 2002 baseball season, when we would start mostly juniors and sophomores along with a couple of very talented freshmen, was to be our turnaround season. In preparation of a long run of success, I planned a retreat just before our season to build camaraderie and leadership among the players. For the first time since coming to SBEC, I had allowed my players to elect captains, three of them. I gave the captains a prominent role at the retreat to give them a greater platform from which to lead our team. I had planned every part of the weekend to build our players first as young men and then as baseball players. And then it all blew up.

**

My assistant coach and I began meeting with individual players, beginning with the captains. We talked about roles on the team, individual strengths, and areas for improvement. After each conversation each player was blindfolded and led into another room. There, the captains led the player to do a trust fall. After the trust fall, that player would join in catching the succeeding players who came into the room.

After each of the players had engaged in conversation with the coaches and completed the trust fall, we had a large group session where we laid out our vision for the team. The players enjoyed free time after that. They went on a snipe hunt with the players who had never been on such a "hunt." Since the land around the retreat center was unfamiliar to the players and since my assistant coach was a coon hunter, each group carried tracking devices so that they wouldn't wander too far from the house. The air was full of laughter...and the crude guy humor that you might have expected. Nobody slept much that Sunday night since the following day was a school holiday.

The next morning, we cooked breakfast and prepared to return home. While I was cleaning the kitchen, I was informed that one of the players had hit his head on the hard floor in another room on the other end of the house. He had been wrestling and gone to the floor too hard. This group of players wrestled even more than most high school guys, but this freshman boy had never joined in before. He had a history of concussions, so we called his parents, and they met us halfway to take him to the hospital and make sure he was okay. By the time we met them, he was talking clearly and seemed to be fine. The rest of us went home to sleep the rest of our holiday away.

Late Monday afternoon, I answered a phone call from my high school principal. He informed me that the parents of the boy who had hit his head wanted to meet with us before school on Tuesday. He warned me that this would not be good. That wasn't surprising, given that they had had issues with every coach at our school who had coached their son. But it was worse than I could have imagined.

***

The freshman baseball player had not suffered any lasting damage to his head, but his parents were looking to lay blame for the accident on someone. At the meeting the next morning, I found myself at the end of the constantly wagging finger of the dad for an hour or so. Between some accusations that would later prove to be true and some outlandish exaggerations, he threatened lawsuits against me, against the school, and against my church (who owned the retreat center). He let my principal know, in no uncertain terms, that he expected me to be fired by the end of the day.

I discovered that the captains of the team had become bored by the end of our series of player meetings and trust falls. They, along with some of the other players, decided to begin a very unsanctioned initiation of freshman by giving them "swirlies" in the toilet in the back of the area where the trust falls were staged.

The snipe hunt was also brought into question. According to the accusations, my assistant coach and I had "hazed" the players by dropping them off in the middle of the woods for them to find their way back. We had let them stay out there in the cold until the early hours of the morning and—somewhere along the way— whipped some of them with barbed wire. In reality, the snipe hunt was the players' idea, one they had after midnight. They carried the tracking devices and were never more than a few minutes walk from the house. One player did have a scrape on his arm from a brush with a barbed wire fence, which we treated with soap, water, and a Band-Aid.

Throughout the day, several of players were called into the school office to give their versions of what happened over the weekend. As the day wore on, word of the charges against me and my assistant coach and some of the players made its way down the halls of the school. One after another, players came to me and asked, "Coach, what's going on?!? What they're saying is not the way it happened!"

**

At the end of that very long day, I called one of my closest friends and told him that I urgently needed to get together with him to pray that night. He said he would call me back in a few moments. When he did, he told me his family had dinner plans with another family and offered no alternative time. I hung up the phone and entered into the one of the loneliest times of my life. I can see now that the Lord was isolating me for a reason.

**

Some of the issues surrounding the retreat gone bad were easy to sort out and conclude. The three captains were stripped of their leadership roles. Apologies were made for joking gone too far. I was suspended from coaching my team for the remainder of the week. I would appear before the school board so that they could determine if they deemed further action necessary.

Ultimately, the board decided to reinstate me with several stipulations. First-year players could no longer be burdened with carrying equipment back and forth to practice, as had been our practice since I had arrived at the school—this was now considered hazing. For three classes of players who had paid their dues—some of them with so few in their class that they made two trips each way every practice—this was not well received. I understood the reasoning behind the decision, what with the attempts of the players to institute their own initiation ritual and all. However, the school board wasn't there for the daily smirks from a couple of the freshman players as they quickly grabbed the scantest of equipment and left the heavier equipment for the older players. This called for no small amount of restraint from the veteran players...or their parents.

Another stipulation from the board was the presence of a school administrator at each of our games, home and away. I was actually excited about this one. We had worked very hard to establish the SBEC baseball program, and this would give our administration the opportunity to witness the growth of our program as we overcame the obstacles now in front of us.

***

Our season-opening tournament was in Corinth, Mississippi. We were already significantly behind in our preparation for the season and were playing teams from Mississippi whose season started two weeks before ours did. We took our lumps in the tournament, but at least we were finally playing baseball. On our last playing day of the week, we checked out of our hotel to many compliments from the front desk. They welcomed us to stay in their hotel any time we returned to Corinth. The team received similar compliments from the restaurant next door to the hotel where we ate several meals.

That afternoon, before returning home, we were asked to stay to play an extra junior varsity game. To a team struggling to catch up to where the others were, this was a welcomed opportunity. The problem was, our assigned administrator for the week had already left the complex to return home. What could happen in an insignificant JV game, right? Plenty.

The home plate umpire struggled a bit with the strike zone during the entire game. He was a big fellow reminiscent in his physique—if not his umpiring skills—of several major league umpires from a generation ago. Our accusatory parents were in attendance and proceeded to deride this poor umpire the entire game. Most comments were laced with the epitaph "Fatty." This was an interesting choice for a term of derision from a man not exactly in top physical condition himself. When the umpire's father, a senior citizen who happened to be attending the game, turned and asked him to stop, the two almost came to blows. Of course, our school administrator was no longer present to witness the incident.

Upon our return to school after spring break week, I was called into the office again to discuss why the team had been nearly kicked out of our hotel for rowdy behavior. That was the word that had somehow reached our school administration. I'm glad I had witnesses to the hotel staff's compliments on our behavior, not to mention the presence of our designated administrator to dismiss that accusation as unfounded.

Smaller incidents continued to happen throughout the year without reprisal to the parents who continued to publicly mull over their decision of whether or not to file a lawsuit. A teacher heard the mother telling a sixth grade basketball parent that she didn't know how the other lady could let her son play junior high basketball for me the following year. After the only senior on the team threw a no-hitter and struck out every opposing batter, she made a snide comment to him belittling the achievement as he walked back to his vehicle with his father after the game.

I grew weary of these shenanigans, but I knew that I had to bear some of this burden on behalf of many of my players who were still seething about what they deemed unfair circumstances. I had to take the high road on their behalf. We were all walking a tightrope—administrators, coaches, players, and parents. I felt it best for all of us to ride out the storm and keep our focus on getting better as a baseball team. Lost in the midst of much of the chaos was a potentially good young baseball team that still had its best baseball to come over the next two years.

During all of the crazy months of February and March 2002, there were times that I didn't know whether or not I would have the choice of keeping my job. I planned to weather the circumstances and continue doing this job that the Lord had taken and then given back as long as the choice was mine. I did not even strongly consider walking away from my team—at first—as tempting as it might have been to do so for my own personal relief. That is, until the chest pains began.

***

Unlike the Hernando drama eight years earlier, I told Loretta every detail of what was going on at SBEC. We prayed together and worked through much confusion together. I had tried to save her from as much as I could from the accusations at Hernando, knowing that they would hurt her maybe even more than they were hurting me. This time, though, she knew everything. When I woke up on a Monday morning with unusual tightness in my chest, she encouraged me to see a doctor.

I was able to get an immediate appointment with a doctor whose son was a sophomore on our team. He had me go through the usual preliminary checks and asked the usual thousand questions or so to determine the source of the chest pains and their severity. When none of those registered a concern, I told him, "You know, Doc, I have been going through a little stress lately."

He put down his clipboard and transitioned from doctor to friend. "Is it ever going to end, Coach?" he asked.

I did not intend to voice the response that I did. I had not made the decision yet—at least I thought I hadn't—but I heard myself saying, "Yeah, it's going to end real soon."

"You're leaving, aren't you?"

I told him that leaving was a very real possibility but that I didn't want the team to know until after the season. They had been through enough upheaval already. I didn't want to add to it. He gave me some anti-depressants to help me with the chest pains for the next few weeks until I could announce my decision.

The next few days felt artificial, as if I was sleepwalking

through them. I have always been extremely opposed to the use of anti-depressants as a mechanism to avoid facing difficult circumstances and choices. Yet there I was, avoiding one of my own. A seemingly inane parent meeting was the final straw that led me to change my mind.

***

The world of private school athletics typically involves several conversations every season with parents about their kids' playing time. Some parents assume that their tuition costs ensure their child's inclusion in his or her extracurricular activities of choice. Some hold to the philosophy that a player's equal playing time was more important than the team's competing to win. Others simply hold a disingenuous view of their child's abilities as compared to others on the team.

I had learned to dance the delicate dance of complimenting a player's athletic abilities and character qualities while informing those who were partially paying my salary that he simply was not good enough to receive more playing time for our team. My meeting that day was with the parents of one of my junior players and the president of the school. The young man was one of the most talented players on the team. He was also one of the most un-coachable players I had ever attempted to coach. He had earned a starting position for two consecutive years and lost it when other players outperformed him.

The meeting that day was very cordial and non-accusatory. These parents actually went out of their way to let me know that they supported me in all the other circumstances of that year. They just wanted very badly for their son to play. I understood that. I wanted him to play, too, but I couldn't continue to start him when others were getting the job done and he was not.

Something clicked within me during the parent meeting. To this day I can't really identify what it was, but I somehow knew that the time had come for my resignation. I walked back to my office and began to type my letter of resignation with at least a partial understanding of the emotion surrounding its crafting. All during the process, I begged the Lord to stop me if I was going against His desire for my life. I had Loretta's blessing to resign, but I didn't want to take just take the easy out. I had already made it through the worst of the storm, but this felt right.

I did not sense an urge to stop, so I printed three copies of my resignation and distributed the letters to my athletic director, my high school principal, and the school president. Our athletic director was in the cafeteria when I found him. He read the letter, nodded, and told me he would be submitting his own resignation by the end of the school year. I left the other letters and jumped on a bus to drive my team to our afternoon games against Briarcrest in Cordova, Tennessee, about an hour away.

***

My assistant coach was a volunteer at the school but had invested deeply in the players on the team. He had coached most of them as junior high players at the school and as high school players on our summer league team. He had recently told me about an opportunity he had to finish his degree and learn from one of the best college coaches in our state. We decided to go ahead and make our announcements after the varsity game that day, as word of my resignation would certainly leak by the following day. He would address the team first and I would follow.

Our team had struggled back from our early-season struggles to about an even won-loss record. There had been some highs when the emerging talent on our team appeared ready to blossom and some lows, reminders that our team was both young and still a team in chaos. The game that day had great potential in either direction. We were facing a good Briarcrest team on the road with a chance to show our mettle or show...whatever it was we showed that day in a 24-1 loss. The result matched the mood of the coaches.

After the game we met with our dejected squad in the middle of the field, out of earshot of the players' parents. Gary went first, as planned, and the reaction of the players was predictable. They knew that good young assistant coaches don't stay in one place very long on their way to an eventual head coaching job. They move along quickly as opportunities arise. While the players would miss him, they understood his decision.

When I followed with the announcement that I had turned in my letter of resignation that day, I thought I was going to have to break up a fight. The eyes of the players who had shown the most restraint throughout the season flared toward the player at the center of the turmoil. I continued to take the high road in front of my team and told them they had a choice as to how to finish out the season. I honestly didn't know how much I had left to give, so the challenge was as much for me as it was for them.

**

I have never been more proud of a group of players for how they responded. We became a team on a mission, going on the longest winning streak I ever enjoyed as a coach. Coaches from teams we had played earlier in the season could not believe the transformation that had taken place since we had first played them...or that I had resigned.

We were still riding that winning streak into a first-of-its-kind unofficial small schools championship. SBEC and other local private schools planned a major sports festival for all the spring sports from small private schools across Tennessee. The day of the tournament came, and so did the rains. Cancellation was imminent, but many of these teams had traveled hours from eastern Tennessee to participate. Finally, though, the skies cleared and we furiously prepared the baseball and softball fields for competition.

Though we had once again gone undefeated through our small schools district schedule, a team from east Tennessee was the odds-on favorite to win. At least that was what we continued to hear throughout the day from the other site for baseball pool play at another local school. Saturday afternoon came and, with it, the baseball championship between SBEC and St. Andrew's. Both teams had played three games and were short on pitching, but both starters looked equal to the task in the first couple of innings of a close game. In the bottom of the third inning, though, we broke through in a big way and cruised to a 10-0 championship victory in run-rule fashion.

The tournament committee named six of our players to the all-tournament team. One of the players awarded all-tournament status was walking off with a much-deserved medal around his neck when a certain player's mother—I'll let you guess which one—stopped him to say, "You might have that around your neck, but you still suck!" And you know what, it didn't even matter by that point in the season.

***

The regional playoffs against the larger teams in the state-sanctioned playoffs came next. We would have to win three games against the larger schools to advance to the sectional round. We lost an early game but won two and faced perennial power Christian Brothers with a berth in the sectional playoff on the line. We entered the game with a great deal of confidence and competed for a while but ultimately bowed out of the tournament one game short. Still, we had advanced further than any small school ever had. The baseball banquet after the season was a quiet affair. Sixteen players out of 20, along with their parents, came to the awards dinner. Two of the absent players had issues with playing time, and the other two were the ones who caused much of that season's dissension. I was able to walk around the tables and address each player individually. They were a team that showed great resilience, and I was grateful to be able look into each of their eyes, to congratulate them on their success in the face of overwhelming circumstances, and to tell them I loved them.

***

The year after I left, the team led by many of these same players not only advanced past the regional tournament to the sectional but won their sectional game and advanced to the state championship tournament. There, they knocked off the defending champion and finished third in the state.

The TSSAA finally officially split the private schools into large and small divisions for the playoffs a few years later, and SBEC won its first baseball state title in 2008. Though all of the players that I coached had graduated by that time, I felt a sense of accomplishment in that state championship. The players that I had coached for eight years at the school had laid a foundation for the group that would later win it all.

More than that, they had faced what surely must have seemed overwhelming circumstances early in their careers and learned to overcome. I have never really liked the phrase "the game of life" that many coaches use because I consider life more significant than any game. I am a big proponent, however, of the value of sports in a young person's life. I constantly challenged my players of all ages and in all the sports I coached to appreciate that they were learning life's lessons through a game; others around the world were learning those lessons through much more trying circumstances.

I still don't fully understand why God asked for my job, gave it back, and then called me away after walking through one of the most difficult times in my life. I would have willingly left when He first asked for my job. I had much more to learn through the fire of that last season, and I suppose I wouldn't have learned what I did from it any other way. I had to choose to trust the Lord's plan.

As the following years went by, I looked back on parts of the saga that I wished I had handled differently. I learned much about life myself, lessons I would need for the road on which God would lead me. The most prominent lesson for me from the baseball season of 2002 was to keep moving toward our common goal in the midst of not understanding why life was unfolding as it was. That's the essence of faith, don't you think?

***

Hebrews 12:1-2

Therefore, since we are surrounded by so great a cloud of witnesses, let us also lay aside every weight, and sin which clings so closely, and let us run with endurance the race that is set before us, looking to Jesus, the founder and perfecter of our faith, who for the joy that was set before him endured the cross, despising the shame, and is seated at the right hand of the throne of God.

9 HANDS IN THE AIR

I reached the point where I felt like God was asking me in my spirit, "Will you trust Me until the money absolutely runs out?" He had been faithful—more than faithful—to meet our needs in the past, and I didn't see why He would ruin his perfect track record. Plus, like Peter in John 6:68, I didn't know to whom else I would turn. So I answered that yes, I would trust Him even if our money absolutely ran out.

***

The school year and my coaching and teaching career ended in late May of 2002. I did not have another job in place, so I set out to pick up whatever work I could. The more odd jobs I could pick up here and there, the longer my two remaining checks from the school would stretch. That was important because just a couple of months after I stepped out on faith, the Lord presented us with an unexpected surprise: we were going to have another baby!

Drew Michael Ainsworth was born in April of 2003, and—other than breaking Loretta's tailbone during delivery—he was an easy baby. He showed a tremendous athleticism during his stay in the hospital, delivering a stream of urine two cribs over to the poor kid who resided there. That has been a source of pride for his big brother, who saw him do it. Drew ate well and slept through the night quickly. In the midst of financial instability, we were suddenly a family of five.

***

I worked for a couple of months installing glass, for a week on a tool truck, for several months selling wholesale club memberships, and for the better part of a year brokering freight. I mowed a couple of yards regularly, and I substituted on various newspaper routes when I had the opportunity. I wasn't making the money I did before, but with a very tight budget, the remainder of the school checks helping out, and no debts besides our mortgage, we made it. But I couldn't keep up the pace.

***

I had been meeting every Friday morning with a group of men in a local accountant's office, and they had been tracking our story. This group was a safe place to talk about my situation, to be challenged, and to ask for prayer. I drew great encouragement from that men's group for that season of life. What I didn't know is that several others in the group were watching my faith move in anticipation of making their own. Soon, my faith story that had been confined largely to that accountability group and my family small group would go public. I was asked to share my "in progress" faith story in front of our whole church.

I prepared my testimony for the church even as the bank account was swirling toward empty. As I prepared my story, though, I had to add an unexpected last sentence or two. Just days before I spoke, I landed a job with an actuarial firm. A church member who worked there had given me a heads up about the job, and I was grateful to get it. I knew that it would not be the start of a new career, but it would pay the bills while I looked for something more in line with how I was geared.

After speaking at church the following Sunday morning, I also met a man whom I had never seen before and whose name I only discovered later. He told me he appreciated my words and shook my hand. As he walked away, I opened my hand to find a $100 bill. (So that's what it feels like to be a college football player....) I never saw him again, but I came to understand that he was in the middle of a faith move of his own. That day, I thought he might have been an angel.

***

I began the job at Watson Wyatt, knowing that in the grand scheme of my life, it would be a minor blip. However, it was nice to be able to go to work and earn a regular paycheck, at least for a season. Loretta and I were able to relax just a little from the financial pressures of the previous two years. Though I was not building a career in the financial services industry, I was being prepared for a new career. I just didn't know it yet.

Several notable memories stand out from this time period of my life. I began to lead my first small group at church. My church softball team won our first state championship. We built our second house and moved to within six years of complete debt freedom. I went with my softball team on my first mission trip. The road toward that trip began with a heartbreaking phone call that I received one day at my cubicle at Watson Wyatt.

***

The call came from Mike, one of my softball teammates. Another of our teammates and my longtime friend, Cary McRae, had been taking his son and daughter to school that morning, just as he did practically every school day. Someone ran a red light, plowing into the side of Cary's truck. Mike didn't know all the details but informed me that Cary's daughter, Madison, was banged up but would be okay. Cary was hurt worse and was in the Regional Medical Center (The Med) dealing with broken ribs and other assorted injuries. His ten-year-old son, Taylor, was hurt the worst, and all Mike could tell me in that initial call was that the outlook was not good. He would call back as soon as he knew more details.

I immediately began to pray for the whole family, especially for Taylor. The waiting between phone calls was excruciating, and I wasn't going to be able to accomplish anything at work, so I eventually took the rest of the day off and drove across town to LeBonheur Children's Hospital. Mike met me in the lobby with an update, a bleak one. Taylor's doctors were giving the family no hope that he would survive the accident.

Cary was right across the street from LeBonheur trying his best to find out any information he could about Taylor. In his heart of hearts, he already knew. Nothing would deter him from gaining his release from The Med, but that did not come quickly. As Cary's wife, Stacey, waited anxiously for news from those attending to Taylor, I was in the first group that was able to get in to visit Cary. That's when it became obvious to me that God was carrying this family in such a way that it would astound us all.

Taylor passed away in the early hours of the following morning. Cary and Stacey were by his side, having said their goodbyes. I had said mine the previous afternoon. My pain certainly didn't compare to his family's, but I was devastated on several levels. I mention them because of how they speak to Taylor's legacy in my family to this day.

Cary and Stacey and I had been friends for many years, and I grieved for their incomprehensible loss. Taylor had been my buddy, too. As the catcher on our softball team, I required very few warm-up tosses, so I waited until everybody else had started throwing before I began to loosen my arm. Once Taylor's baseball season was over, he was always in our dugout with his glove ready to volunteer to be my throwing partner. I considered that special even before the accident took my throwing partner from me. Taylor was such a servant at church to kids younger than he was, too. My son Garrett was a few years younger than Taylor and very shy. Taylor took Garrett under his wing and gave him an older kid to look to as a role model.

I grieved on all those levels then and sometimes even now as I write with a large lump in my throat and tears in my eyes. The next few months would teach me more about God and His merciful sovereignty than any other period in my life. I had the privilege of a front row seat to how Cary and Stacey determinedly chose to trust God in the most trying circumstances they could imagine. They offered forgiveness to the other driver, and they demanded that the insurance company not pursue punitive damages. They allowed those who chose to be near them to be close when they were doing well and when they were falling apart.

I am summing up in a only a few paragraphs a story worthy of its own volume, but the faith journey through which the McRaes chose to allow others to be intertwined would lead where none of us could have imagined. For our softball team, Taylor's death changed the way we approached the sport. We began to share our faith with other teams with Cary's testimony usually as the centerpiece. A year after the accident, we traveled to Belize together on a mission trip. It was the first mission trip for most of us and the first of a continuing string of trips to Belize that continues today.

***

That first mission trip was another game changer for me. Most short-term mission trips I had paid attention to were centered on construction. To put it mildly, construction is not my strong suit. I never would have dreamed that my coaching background and my experience conducting baseball skills camps could be used on a mission trip. Yet, as we prepared to lead fast-pitch softball clinics in the elementary schools in the western part of Belize each day and play against local men's teams in San Ignatio at night, I found myself in a leadership role on my very first mission trip.

I've often heard mission trips referred to as "serving the less fortunate." Several people told me that the trip to Belize would make me grateful for what I had. Just two days into this trip, though, I was having a conversation with one of my teammates about how that seemed far too small a purpose. He finished my thought by saying, "I want what they have." What the Belizeans—especially the kids—with whom we interacted had was contentment.

Dozens of children and adults gave their lives to Christ on that first trip. I returned to Belize along with my then-nine-year-old son Garrett and the rest of team the following year. Many more came to know the Lord, and my passion for missions continued to grow. I have not gone back to Belize since 2006, but I have been on a domestic or international mission trip every year since. Every member of my family has been on at least one international trip, and our total number of mission trips is now over 20 and climbing with every passing year.

***

I often think back to that tragic day that Taylor McRae passed away as the kick-start to my getting serious about living for others. I had a chance to ride with Cary and Stacey to a softball tournament in south Mississippi a few months after our first mission trip. They talked very openly about the tension between how God had used Taylor's death for His glory and the longing they felt to have him back. Given the choice, they said, they would always choose to have their son back.

Isn't that the way it is with faith, though—we don't always have our choice of circumstances, but we do choose how we allow God to work through them. Even in our most difficult times, we have a choice of how we respond. That response both reveals where our faith in God really is and stretches that same faith.

Because of Taylor's death and the snowball effect it had on people, hundreds of people became new followers of Christ. Because I was able to see Cary and Stacey's faith journey from up close, I will never be the same. But given the choice, I, too, would take Taylor back.

***

Job 42:15 (NLT)

I had only heard about you before, but now I have seen you with my own eyes.

10 EDGE OF THE DROP

I had been waiting on a reply from Pastor Denny Burt to an offer I had made several weeks prior to the end of 2005. I had volunteered to help write some curriculum for a church-wide small group study that our church had scheduled for the first of the new year. Denny had worked with small groups at some level for years, but that was just one of several roles for him on the church staff. I knew he could use the help. I love to organize projects—you wouldn't guess that by a cursory glance at my desk or the inside of my truck—but I wanted to get started in time to do it right...or let go of the idea if he didn't want the help. I didn't understand the delay.

***

The first Belize trip, along with my continuing leadership of a small group, made me long for a career that made a difference. I had crunched numbers and filled out forms for about as long as I could stand, but I was trying to make the most of ministry opportunities at Watson Wyatt as they arose. I walked with one of my younger co-workers through a very difficult part of his life and mentored three colleagues through the advantages of becoming debt free. (One of those guys bought as many Xbox 360's as he could during the Christmas season the year they were first available and re-sold them on eBay. He fully funded his $10,000 emergency fund in one week and left the company not long afterward to go to work for Dave Ramsey's organization.)

Some of my most rewarding times at Watson Wyatt were during late lunches on the patio overlooking the Southwind TPC golf course. I would wait until others had eaten and quickly devour my daily fare of a peanut butter and jelly sandwich, apple, and Nutty Bar in order to use the rest of my lunchtime to prepare for that week's small group lesson. I began to feel an ache to do more in ministry, and I prayed that God would lead me in that direction.

When considering the type of ministry I wanted to pursue, I felt drawn in two directions. One route came from a marriage study I had developed and led in my church small group. It was highly interactive and adventurous with a great deal of team building at various levels. I thought it would make a meaningful and fun weekend retreat, so I started laying out some plans.

The other direction toward which I moved was a non-profit organization designed to help coaches not only teach sports through proper fundamentals but also to assist them in applying the lessons learned in sports to their young players' lives. I eventually called that would-be non-profit organization Right Way Sports. Right Way Sports was the idea I felt most equipped to pursue. I had a number of thoughts, sketches, articles—a whole binder full of ideas waiting to be implemented. I paid a graphic designer to develop a logo and was very pleased with his design. I ordered letterhead, envelopes, and business cards with my new logo and began the process of garnering 501(c)(3) non-profit status. With the paperwork ready to be filled out and submitted, the direction of my life and my career took an unexpected turn.

***

Near the end of 2005, I sensed that the end of my actuarial career had come. In a shuffling of employees, I was being moved from the small pension plan team to the medium team. On the small team, where we dealt with plans of less than 200 or so employees, I could cover for my inadequacies in our computer systems reasonably well. I could see when the numbers just didn't look right and could often compute in my head what the ballpark numbers ought to be and work toward them. On the medium team, the numbers would be too big for me to do that, and my skills on the computer programs we used would need to be much more keen.

I had enough paid time off remaining to use the days between Christmas and New Year's as vacation. I sensed the need to get away for at least an entire day to pray and seek God's direction. The time had come for a move but in which direction? I couldn't process all the thoughts in the midst of the hustle of life, particularly as we approached Christmas. I planned a day of fasting and prayer for a few days after Christmas. I had the perfect place for such a retreat.

***

Loretta had said that she would never build another house. However, she kept a notebook of ideas and of sub-contractors she would use...just in case. A couple of years before this time, DeSoto Central High School had opened a few miles north of us. The new school opened to such rave reviews that people began flooding into the area, sending property values in our area skyrocketing. We decided to take advantage of what could very well be a short window of opportunity and build again with the idea that, this time, we might just be able to build it and be free of a house note forever.

Finding a lot to build on turned out to be more of a challenge than we had imagined. We were looking for an acre or more but with much less lawn care than our current two-acre lot. We set what we thought was a reasonable price range and began to scour the county for new subdivisions that met our criteria. After weeks of looking, we finally found a neighborhood in our price range. It was further from town than we wanted to be, the lots were three (mostly mow-able) acres, and we would have the additional expense of digging a well. No thanks, we decided.

Discouraged, we drove back toward our house, meandering to other potential new neighborhoods when we found the perfect lot in a small, mostly undeveloped neighborhood. We signed a contract on it the next day for just a little more than we had budgeted. Others discovered the neighborhood about the same time, and prices on the lots increased soon afterward to more than we could have paid.

We had not yet begun construction of our house at the end of 2005, so it was still a mostly wooded lot surrounded by other wooded lots. This was where I would bring a chair, my Bible, and a journal for a day of fasting and prayer regarding my future. More specifically, I wanted to know God's plan for my future. As with my time in the coaching profession, I could tell He was leading me away from something. I would need to seek Him to discover which direction to move—marriage retreats or Right Way Sports. Or both. A phone call a week before Christmas complicated matters.

***

The call was from Denny Burt. I expected our conversation to center around the curriculum for the quickly approaching small group term. Instead, he asked me to meet with him and our church's administrator before church that Wednesday night. That was odd, I thought, but with so much more to consider in the midst of the Christmas season, I didn't give the meeting too much thought. On that Wednesday night, they asked me to pray through entering a process that could ultimately lead to my coming on our church's staff as the new small groups pastor.

My gut-level first response was, "Great...now I have three directions to pray through." That day in the woods was well timed, for sure, but now it had become more complicated. I could see that the writing and organizational skills that I possessed would bring value to my church's leadership. I had served as a deacon during some of the most trying times in our church's history. Loretta and I had been married in our church, and it was the only church my children had ever known. My growing role within the small groups ministry seemed to be outgrowing the number of volunteer hours I could commit to it. The decision might have seemed like a slam dunk.

But what about the other directions in which I had sensed the Lord's leading? What about this burgeoning entrepreneurial spirit that was welling up in me? As someone who grew up hearing that good jobs equaled secure jobs with good benefits, the thought of making my own way as the head of a new non-profit both exhilarated me and scared me to death. I was intrigued by the dream of what could be. One part of my decision was clear: whichever path I chose, I wanted to give value to the lives of others.

***

I found a clearing in the bottom of a ravine to set up camp for the day. Protected from the wind and out of view from anyone driving through the neighborhood, I purposed to meet with God until I felt clear about His direction for my life. I started a fire and warmed myself by its heat and by the Word of God as it began to stir my soul. At the beginning of the day, I would have told you that Right Way Sports had a small advantage over my other two options. I had developed that idea more than the marriage retreat idea and had considered it longer. Besides, I had money invested in that idea, having already bought stationery and business cards.

As the day wore on, I weighed the risk of Right Way Sports versus taking a staff position. I did not want to choose the safer, more intuitive option because of my fears or even my preferences. I gave the options to the Lord and asked Him to differentiate between them. The chill of the morning gave way to a peaceful afternoon, and God began to bring me peace in the direction of moving toward becoming the next small groups pastor at CHC.

One question I asked in my journal during that afternoon in the woods was what my family's lives would look like if I took the small groups position. I had no sooner written those words than I heard a shuffling in the clearing above where I was. A very large deer walked majestically across the ridge, totally unaware of my presence. I reached slowly for my camera that I had brought just in case I had such an opportunity. I slowly brought it to my eye to focus on this magnificent creature. I zoomed in and pressed the button, which caused the camera to blurt out a "beep beep." Startled, the deer bolted for the cover of the deeper woods but not before I captured her photo as a reminder of my question to the Lord.

I returned to the thought I had just written in my journal about my family's life as a pastor's family. What did the deer's appearance mean? Would being a small groups pastor be a regal, majestic experience? Or would it be wild and fleeting? Likely both, I thought.

***

I returned from my retreat content with my decision. After a little over a month of meetings, evaluations, and conversations, I became the new small groups pastor at Colonial Hills Church. The spring term of groups was just underway, and a major missions conference (in which I lined up small groups for our visiting missionaries to visit) took place my second weekend on staff. There was no time for much of an orientation. I hit the ground running.

***

My small group at that time consisted mainly of our softball team and families. We were preparing for the second trip to Belize when my call became public, and I shared much of the backstory of my decision the night of the announcement. I talked about God's call away from coaching and not really into anything else immediately. As more of transition statement than one looking for a response, I said at one point, "Y'all probably thought I was crazy, but..." I paused when I saw heads nodding around the room.

I had not thought too much about what other people were thinking of my faith move. Theirs were not the voices I needed to be focusing on anyway, but now—four years after leaving teaching and coaching—I began to realize what our situation must have looked like from the outside looking in. Walking away from a career without having something else in place may not have been a wise move—not the direction I would immediately counsel others to even consider—but it was clearly the direction God was leading. Just like when the children of Israel were trapped between the Red Sea and the quickly approaching Egyptian army, He had a road already mapped out. We just had to trust that it was there...somewhere.

How did Moses' successor, Joshua, feel when he stood before the captain of the Lord's army? This was the powerful archangel who gave him the exceptionally unconventional battle plan that he was to use to conquer Jericho. March around the city and blow trumpets and yell? Suuuurrre... I wonder, though, if he might have felt supreme confidence while in the presence of the Lord. But later, when he tried to communicate the plan to his military leaders, did he feel foolish? I had no doubts about where the Lord was leading my family, but trying to put that into words that others would understand made God's work in my life seem very irrational. It could only be described in the context of faith.

I cannot even imagine what our "four years in the wilderness," as we now describe this period of our lives, must have been like for Loretta. As the leader of our family, I was doing my best to describe how the Lord was leading me, but she had to choose to trust my leadership in our home even when I didn't fully understand what in the world was going on in our lives. She made a statement just on the other side of God making the next step clear that I will never forget.

She said, "I haven't always understood where you were leading us. I haven't always *agreed* with where you were leading us. But I have never, for one moment, regretted submitting to your leadership." That was as affirming as any statement anyone has ever made to me. It also made me realize just how much responsibility I was shouldering as the leader of my family. My choices mattered—both in practical and deeply spiritual ways—not just for the moment but extending far beyond just my generation.

***

Psalm 77:19 (NLT)

Your road led through the sea, your pathway through the might waters—a pathway no one knew was there.

11 FREEFALLING

"Make my heart leap."

With those words, Pastor Rick smiled and ushered me out of his office. I walked down the hall knowing that—one way or the other—I was about to engage in another defining moment in my life. I wondered if God might be ushering me into another faith move...and if I was ready for it.

***

The first few years of small groups ministry were a blur. When I was hired, five seminary classes made up the extent of my formal ministry training. About half of our church staff at that time had seminary degrees, and the other half of us had prepared for ministry through practical training in different ministries of our church. I had an understanding with our leadership team that I would return to school to finish my formal training. However, as ministry life quickly consumed much of my time, neither they nor I pushed much for me to pursue further higher education. I had much to learn on the job, and I leaned heavily on some of the other pastors.

The skills that I possessed that were attractive to our leadership team were my writing and teaching skills, along with my ability to organize and communicate vision to a team. As I found my footing as a staff pastor, I began to use those skills to re-write outdated and verbose training materials, to communicate a consistent vision for small groups within the vision overall church vision, and to organize and write curriculum for our groups.

***

The fall of the housing market in 2008 brought changes to our church as it did in practically every segment of the economy. The stress of a shrinking budget made for some difficult decisions. The unavoidable ministry cuts were likened to progressively "cutting the fat," "cutting the meat," and "cutting the bone."

My family lived on a tight budget already, so the economic slide didn't impact us immediately. We moved into our new house in the same year that I came on staff, and our payoff date was in sight from the beginning. However, as gas prices, grocery prices, and health insurance costs continued to skyrocket, we felt the pinch. After the ministry cuts began, any hope of cost-of-living pay raises was replaced by the gratitude of still having a job.

***

In 2010, I read a little orange book called *Radical*, David

Platt's manifesto on how to live life focused on the kingdom of God rather than the American dream. I felt more and more alive as I turned each page. I had let the cares of life and ministry and budgets cloud what was most important, but this was beyond buildings and programs. This was truly living for something greater than myself. My family committed to do the Radical Experiment in 2011. For one year we would (1) pray for the entire world, (2) read through the entire Word, (3) sacrifice our money for a specific purpose, (4) spend our time in another context, and (5) commit our lives to a multiplying community.

***

The year 2011 was one of the most freeing years of my life. I remember a disaster relief trip that came up suddenly, and I didn't have to check the bank account before responding. Yes, I would go. I asked my family who wanted to go, and Ashton and Drew took me up on the offer. Ashton wanted to bring a friend and I was able to tell her sure, bring your friend; it won't cost her a thing. We spent most of the day in a small town in northeast Alabama organizing an entire National Guard Armory full of food, water, furniture, clothes, toys, and various other items for tornado victims.

At the end of the day, Drew and I decided to tackle a large room about knee high in mostly unmatched shoes. He was eight years old at the time, so I decided to make a game of matching shoes. The turquoise pumps with four-inch heels were easy to match (with one another, that is, not necessarily with a need that we could fathom). As we began this seemingly overwhelming task, others who had completed (or become bored with) their tasks glanced in to see what we were doing. We looked like we were having a good time, so they joined us. Before we left for home later that afternoon, our growing group of helpers had matched almost all the shoes in the entire room and sorted them according to size.

This was a great picture of what the Lord was teaching me about not just continuing to serve Him locally and globally but about the importance of bringing others alongside me. In the smaller picture, we were simply sorting shoes and organizing food, clothes, and other household items. In the bigger picture, we were coming alongside three extremely overwhelmed little old ladies who were tackling the organization and distribution of a mammoth amount of relief supplies that continued to arrive by the truckload in a town that had gone unnoticed by government organizations. (As we were leaving town, we saw FEMA vehicles arriving.) Bigger than that, though, one of the men that we struck up a relationship with said that our team was instrumental in his returning to church, where he gave his life to Christ a few months later.

In so many ways, the Radical Experiment was a turning point in my life. Though I fell short of some of the goals, discipleship became a primary objective for me. I began to meet weekly with a young man in my small group, walking through a discipleship track that our missions pastor had assembled. Jacob and I talked often of good intentions and the danger of leaving them on the table.

During one of these discussions, he coined the term *rollover days*. Inspired by rollover minutes on a cell phone plan, rollover days happen when good intentions are left undone, and one day turns into the next turns into the next turns into the next. Before long, time has passed, nothing worthwhile has been accomplished, and windows of opportunity have closed.

***

One area that I became determined not to allow to "roll over" one more year was in reading the entire Bible together in small groups. I had worked for months to lead our groups in that direction in 2010. However, a last-minute decision (from an organizational standpoint) from our senior pastor sent us another direction. We changed course and did a recovery-related study that proved successful and life changing to many of our people, myself included.

In the fall of 2011, I enlisted the help of several volunteers in our church to help me make a systematic reading of the Bible attractive and fruitful to our people. The women's ministry had undertaken a chronological study of the Word that same year. I met with the leaders who walked their ministry through what was a paradigm-shifting course change. I wanted to know their best practices, but I was also concerned about some of the ladies resisting a second year through the chronological Bible study.

Lynn and Cyndi assured me that the excitement I had been hearing about the chronological Bible study was indeed widespread. They predicted—correctly, as it turned out—that the ladies who were engaged in the study would be eager for its church-wide launch. They took me back to their point of decision, though, and that gave me pause for concern.

Lynn pointed out that they "had to go back to zero" in choosing this direction. For well over a decade, she said, the ladies' Tuesday morning Bible studies had operated in the same fashion. Six studies were offered each term. On the first day of each new spring or fall term, a table with materials for all of the potential classes was set up, and the ladies signed up for the classes they wanted to take. Most made their decisions by staying with a particular teacher they liked or by choosing the most attractive book cover of the available classes.

The chronological Bible study would operate much differently. Each week, the ladies would meet together to watch a video related to the eras of Scripture and then break out into small groups where they would discuss that week's Bible reading. The leaders knew God had led them in this direction but had no way of knowing what the response from the ladies would be. They had to be willing to "go back to zero."

I was not afraid to "go back to zero" with the entire small groups ministry to give our people a foundation from which they could more deeply study and obey God's Word. I felt strongly that God was leading me in that direction and that He had been for some time. As a church we had long since begun to reach the very people we had purposed and prayed to reach, those who had no church background and very little knowledge of the Word of God. This study would give those unfamiliar with the Bible a foundation from which to build. In addition, our small group members would see the bigger story of God's plan of redemption, revealed over time, as we studied the eras of Scripture and how each fit into God's story.

I did my homework on these types of studies in other contexts and found a church that had successfully incorporated a yearlong Bible study into both the personal and corporate facets of their people's lives. I solicited the assistance of Jeff Witt, one of our small group leaders who also had a marketing degree. He helped me set up a marketing mix so that we could roll out this massive study in an attractive way to our leaders and to their small groups.

We systematically rolled out our plan first to our senior pastor, then to the rest of the staff, then to our group leaders, and finally to the church at large. Our greatest evangelists for the Bible reading plan was indeed those ladies who had already spent almost a year doing the study. Most marketing experts would agree that word-of-mouth endorsements from satisfied customers are the best advertising you could have, and we had them! For the groups and individuals who engaged in the yearlong Bible study— appropriately dubbed *Engage*—2012 was a year of tremendous growth in God's Word. It was much more eagerly received than it would have if we had attempted to launch it two years prior when I had first planned the study.

As we might have predicted, though, people tended to get behind in their reading, and small group attendance waned once we hit the summer months. To this day, though, my small group and others continue to go back to many of the truths of the bigger picture of God's Word that we encountered in the *Engage* study.

***

The year 2012 brought other paradigm shifts to ministry at

Colonial Hills for all of our staff and for our people. Our senior staff had previously led us in the direction of the multi-site church model. All of our staff members had spent much of 2011 studying and reporting on what this would mean for each of our ministries. Finally, we announced that in addition to our 40-plus-year-old Southaven campus, we would be adding a satellite campus in Hernando, about 10 miles to the south. Our excitement about increased opportunity to reach people in a new area was tempered by the hundreds who left the church within the next few months. This was reminiscent of when we had replaced Sunday school with small groups.

From a small groups standpoint, I had done due diligence and had included several key volunteers in shaping what small groups ministry would look like from one church in two locations. We visited others churches our size or bigger that had successfully implemented small groups ministry into satellite campuses. Most had bigger budgets and larger staffs at those campuses, but we felt like we had drawn enough from their best practices to be able to integrate people into groups successfully at two separate locations.

Much of our plan hinged on volunteer leadership being able to duplicate on each campus what I was then doing at our one campus. I enlisted volunteer campus directors Jeff Witt and Stacy Dodd to take charge of leader meetings, to communicate with leaders during the week, to lead the small groups session of our new members class, and to integrate new people into groups. They were perfect for the roles that they quickly embraced.

During the lead-up to the launch of the new campus, our staff underwent a series of changes. Several pastors left as the staff needs going forward began to shift. Likened to "seats on the bus," some staff pastors were replaced, and other staff positions were left unfilled. The transition time was unsettling for all of us, but changes seemed to be coming too rapidly to spend much time pondering them.

***

Near the end of 2012, I was unexpectedly asked to be a part of a mission trip to Haiti. A young lady in our small group had gone to Haiti earlier in the year with a group of ladies from our church. Their experience and Stephanie's stories that she told to our group made her husband Jacob (the same young man I was meeting with regularly at the time) and I want to go. When a team from Illinois had a couple of extra spots on their team, our missions pastor encouraged us to go.

Before we left, I did a book swap with John Sayger, our student pastor. I had been trying to persuade him to read *Orphanology*, an excellent book about the foundations for orphan care ministry by my friends Tony Merida and Rick Morton. John had been trying to convince me to read *T4T*, by Steve Scott and Ying Kai, a model of discipleship used mainly among unreached people groups. Our exchange of books would play a prominent role in how God would use my trip to Haiti.

A number of factors worked together to make my first trip to Haiti one that would change the course of my ministry and, ultimately, my career beyond the ministry. As we settled in to our home for the next week, Jacob and I felt immediately at ease with our team. Pastor Scott Sims facilitated the team and kept us on task of recording what we saw, what it meant, and what God wanted to do with it. We spent the week working with the most cohesive mission team of which I've ever been a part and hearing their stories as we worked on building a new home for the children of the House of Abraham (HoA).

We spent the week playing with the 13 amazing children who live in the House of Abraham. We worshipped with our brothers and sisters from Haiti, not to mention those from Illinois and Florida. And we built a relationship with HoA director Fenel Bruna, one of the greatest visionary minds that I know.

***

In the chaos of all that was happening around us, God spoke. I realized that almost from the first time I had heard the words *satellite campus* in regard to our church, I had not stopped to take stock of where I was, how I got there, and the changes that I needed to make in my personal life and as the leader of the small groups ministry. Every morning in Haiti, I would rise early to climb the stairs to the roof and spend time with God as the sun rose above the horizon. Every evening between playing with the kids and eating supper and debriefing meetings, I would read. And God would speak.

Every night, I would lie in my bed and listen to praise music. Unable to sleep until the early morning hours because of the heat, I would weep before the Lord in worship for hours. And then He would give me strength to do it all over again the next day. I was like a parched land receiving steady, gentle rain that showed no signs of stopping.

On our last night in Jacmel, I led one of the most humbling ceremonies I have experienced as a believer. When Scott asked me to lead a devotional during the week, I sensed immediately what the Lord wanted me to do. Jacob and I had brought the props that our group would need.

Before we left the United States, we had asked Fenel if there were any specific needs that the children had. He had replied that they needed towels. Our small group takes a "Change It Now" offering every week—no more than a dollar from each person each week—to put toward a gospel-centered cause and to remind us that our spare change is enough to make a difference in someone else's world. We had raised just enough to purchase the towels, but Stephanie and her mom took our gift a step further and monogrammed the towels with the each of the children's names.

On our last night in Haiti, I led a devotion about Jesus washing the disciples' feet. We met on the roof, and the kids were intentionally seated in a circle in the middle of the group. After a few minutes of talking about the passage of Scripture, Fenel brought out a bucket of water and a bar of soap. Every member of the team had chosen one of the children and had that child's towel.

One at a time, a team member would wash one of the children's feet, dry it with that child's new towel, and fold it where he could see his own name on the towel for the first time. Appropriately, that day was the day that many churches around the world recognized as Orphan Sunday.

Here I was, far from home and washing the feet of an orphaned child who could do nothing for me materially. I have never felt more like Christ. First, *Radical*. Then, *Engage*. Then, *Orphanology* and *T4T*. Now this—putting hands and feet to the challenges I was sensing in regard to discipleship. The Lord had my attention, and He was focusing my heart on discipleship, especially among those who had nothing to give but themselves.

As our airplane lifted off from the Port-au-Prince airport to return us to our lives back in the States, I felt something I had not experienced on any of my prior missions trips. I was missing something. Yes, a piece of my heart was still over the mountains in Jacmel, Haiti. I knew that I must return to reconnect with it soon and often.

***

From a small groups standpoint, this direction in which God was leading me fleshed itself out in a discipleship study developed by David Platt and Francis Chan called *Multiply*. At the beginning of the study, I taught two group leaders—Jeff and Stacy, our volunteer small groups directors at each CHC campus—a new method of sharing the gospel that we dubbed "The Kingdom Method." Jeff taught it to our experienced leaders at a retreat. They, in turn, taught it to each of our new leaders. This was the model of discipleship that we wanted our small groups to practice.

The leaders were nervous about trying something new. However, many of our church members had learned multiple methods of sharing the gospel. They just didn't know how to actually do it. I felt that we had discovered a missing element of discipleship: practice. I likened it to a baseball coach teaching his team all about hitting, then writing out a lineup on opening day and expecting his team to be successful. Without the element of practice—practice among those who are on the same side and trying to accomplish the same objective—scores of our people lacked the necessary skills to truly disciple others.

During the five months that our groups did the *Multiply* study, many group leaders and members were sharing their faith like never before. A number of people, including my campus directors and me, led others to Christ using the Kingdom Method. However, not all groups were as enthusiastic about this method of small group ministry. Though the kingdom of God was growing because of the works of those who did engage in this model of discipleship, the overall number involved in groups continued to decline. I had been willing to "go back to zero," but now that the numbers were trending in that direction, I wasn't so confident.

***

In the midst of teaching others to give away what they had learned in their spiritual journeys through this process called discipleship, I became connected with a man who knocked my previous discipleship experiences off kilter. Mark was attempting to re-engage with society after over a decade of near isolation. He lived with his sister, who was also his best friend and one of the only people with whom he had regularly communicated for the past ten years. He rarely ventured out except for visits to the doctor and trips to the grocery store. I wasn't sure why he had picked me to disciple him, other than possibly a recommendation from a mutual friend.

A few months before I met him, Mark was living on disability income but had decided to try his hand at starting an online business. Regular trips to the post office meant frequent interactions with Jim Berggren. Jim is a smiling face and a conversationalist in the midst of the chaos that often describes a large post office. Mark considered him a little chatty for where he was in life, but he eventually came to trust Jim as genuine. Jim recognized a need in Mark's life and one day invited him to our church's Celebrate Recovery (CR) meeting that Friday night, even committing to accompany Mark.

To Mark's own surprise, he found himself at that Celebrate Recovery meeting. There, he met Stacy Dodd. As well as being the Southaven campus small groups director, Stacy is the director of CR and possibly has more energy and enthusiasm than any other human on the planet. Stacy drew Mark in and invited him to his home group and eventually into a one-on-one accountability relationship.

Along the way Mark was offended by a message that Pastor Denny Burt shared one Friday night at CR, one that he felt questioned his boyhood salvation. Angrily, he shared his frustration with God on the back patio of his sister's home that night. The Lord's peace settled on Mark that night and let him know that, indeed, he had never surrendered his life to Jesus. With the best words he could remember from verses learned decades before, Mark gave his life to Jesus that night.

***

Several months passed before Mark showed up in my office. I had met him a couple of times by then, but I knew him more by the reputation of his remarkable story. I gave him the one condition of my commitment to personally disciple him, the same one I had given Jacob a few years earlier: You must actively look to bring someone else alongside you and teach him what you learn from me. Mark agreed and I asked a question of him that set our story in motion. I simply asked, "What's your story?" He chose the long version.

Mark's story is not mine to re-tell, and I would not break his confidence to tell it anyway. Suffice it to say that though we had the common ground of both being students at the University of Southern Mississippi at the same time in the mid- to late-1980's, his life was remarkably different from mine. As he walked me through one dysfunctional era of his life after another, I began to worship the only Source of hope someone caught in such a web has. When he brought his story to the present, he paused and made a simple statement that he hadn't planned on telling me any of that. Then, he said, "But I felt like I could trust you."

Mark and I met weekly as often as we were able for several months after that. He was discovering for the first time how God had uniquely created him. Though he still struggled with reintegration into society and learning to trust others, Mark was taking every occasion to share what he was learning with others. He was becoming increasingly frustrated, though, with the lack of opportunities to disciple others one-on-one. His sister Tammie became his sounding board for everything he was learning, allowing him to practice even though other doors continued to close.

***

I had not met with Mark for several weeks as he battled an extended illness. He was recovering and we were about to reconvene our meetings when I received the tragic message that Mark's sister had been killed in an automobile accident near their home. Tammie had asked him if he wanted to go to Sonic to take advantage of their half-price summer shakes, something they did together several nights a week (and something else we had in common). He tapped out because his back was hurting, but he gave her his shake order and told her he loved her, as he always did. She was turning out of the neighborhood when another vehicle crashed into hers, killing her instantly.

I was asked to preach Tammie's funeral. In the days leading up to the funeral, I began to discover a trail of Mark's influence in repairing a broken family. When he gave his life to Jesus and began to learn about forgiveness and restoration, Mark began to apply it to his family members. As he moved forward in obedience to the Word of God, Tammie moved, too.

Though Mark never considered himself to be discipling Tammie, he was. And she was taking action. She had mended fractured relationships in their family like Mark had. The family told me that if she had passed away just one year earlier, they would have been a mess. When her sudden death happened, though, they were able to celebrate her life with few regrets. Hers became one of the easiest funerals for which I have ever prepared and also one of the most impactful. Her story was the story of redemption, a mirror of God's grand story of redemption.

Eight months after I received the message of Tammie's death, I received with great sadness the message that Mark, too, had passed away. I was deeply saddened that Mark was gone, but I couldn't help but think of the joy that must have filled his soul at his first glimpse of heaven. When I read about the absence of sorrow and pain in heaven, I think about how different Mark's life is there than it was on earth. I counted it a great responsibility to be one of the very few people to whom Mark shared the deepest, darkest parts of his life. I think about what a small window of opportunity that was and how glad I am that I made time for it, even in the midst of one of the most hectic times of my life.

Mark was one of several people that God sent in my direction during those years. These were people that—outside of God's purposely putting me at specific intersections in their lives—I may never have met. Mike faced a choice between his bottle and his family; God allowed me to be a part of the transforming work He has done in Mike in just a few years since. Steve and Stacy wanted to honor God in their marriage and were willing to walk a difficult road to do it. God chose me to challenge them in that direction; today, their impact for the kingdom of God is widespread and profound. I have thanked the Lord often for the privilege of being a part of their stories of radical transformation.

***

For as far back as I can remember in formal small groups ministry at Colonial Hills Church—well before I came on staff as the small groups pastor—dual priorities have been emphasized: community and discipleship. We have said it a couple of different ways over the years: "helping get people saved and helping saved people to grow," then "getting people connected and helping them take the next step toward spiritual maturity." God's regenerative work in people like Mark, Tammie, Mike, Steve, and Stacy rarely happens without the involvement of others to come alongside them to teach them, challenge them, and encourage them.

As I met regularly with my small groups campus directors, a different sort of emphasis in how we communicated the priorities of community and discipleship began to emerge. Rather than as two equal segments of small groups, we recognized discipleship as the ultimate "win" of our ministry and community as the best vehicle to accomplish it. Many of our group leaders, particularly the ones who met with their campus directors each week, embraced this subtle shift and began to do the hard work of making disciples week by week. The overall number of people in small groups, however, continued to decline.

***

A few months after the launch of the new campus, I felt great accomplishment in the leadership development of my campus directors. They were simply doing a remarkable job at their respective church campuses, and the small group leaders had embraced their different styles. I rotated campuses, sitting in on what I claimed from the beginning as their leader meetings. I was able to keep my fingers on the pulse of what was going on at both campuses, but I began to feel like what the corporate world would recognize as mid-level management.

From a more personal standpoint, I wanted to worship on the same campus that my family did every week. That was not going to be possible at least every other week. I also began to feel disheartened by a greeting I began to receive week after week at whichever campus I attended: "Well, hello, stranger!" It was always offered in lighthearted fun, but I was feeling increasingly like a stranger, not on one campus but at two sites.

I thought small groups ministry was as ready as any other to meet the challenges of a new campus with no increase in paid staff presence. I had studied the challenges and, together with Jeff and Stacy, had come up with what we all thought was a workable plan. The united discipleship conference at our Southaven campus to kick off 2013 had been well received. By many measures, the spring term was the most successful of my tenure. However, the number of small groups, new leaders, and new members was not growing. That trend continued into the fall semester. That was a problem.

***

By the end of 2013, I felt the strain of my ministry, both from a pastoral and a personal standpoint. On September 5, 2013, I had scheduled meeting with Pastor Rick Sayger, our senior pastor. He had scheduled the meeting and I was unaware of its purpose, though this was not unusual. I immediately sensed a seriousness about the meeting when I entered to find two other senior staff pastors waiting. Pastor Rick told me that this would not be easy and handed me a letter. The letter communicated his concern over the decline in the small groups ministry and lack of evidence on my part of a strong passion for small group ministry. The letter gave me notice of a 90-day evaluation period that would begin within a week.

I had done the math during our conversation that day and found that the end of 90 days fell two weeks before Christmas. I was shaken by the timing but determined to meet my pastor's admonition to make his heart leap with my enthusiasm for the role to which the Lord had called me eight years earlier. I walked down the hall to my office and set about looking for new ways of doing small groups that would encourage more participation and entice new leaders. I was able to discover some new, trendsetting ways of leading small groups based on advances in technology that were relatively new to the market. This technology certainly had potential but was unlikely to replace old-fashioned face-to-face relationships as the ideal way to disciple people. However, it represented potential to draw people to groups in the first place; hopefully, deeper discipleship would follow.

I felt like I had found at least one of the pieces of the puzzle for which our senior staff was looking. However, at the end of that and each succeeding day of searching for and implementing these new methods, I grew more and more exhausted and dissatisfied with my work. My passion for discipleship wasn't matching up with my role on our church staff. Something just wasn't right.

***

Within a day or two of the September 5 meeting, I reached out to a friend at another church. He had been through a tumultuous pastor search at another church in our area a few years before. Several different people, when they found out I knew him, had spoken highly of his character and integrity through that entire process. He graciously agreed to meet with me very soon after my call.

I told my friend that my desire was not to find someone who would necessarily agree with my feelings but to help me sort through them and walk through the situation with integrity. I stated my desire to stay well or leave well, whatever the Lord allowed or directed. He agreed to help and began to walk me through a process of discovering God's will for me while at the same time walking uprightly and fulfilling my ministry role with purpose for as long as I was in it. He suggested proposing a meeting with Pastor Rick weekly to better understand his desires for my ministry role. He suggested that these meetings might lead us to a place that neither Rick nor I could have ever imagined. He was right.

***

The official 90-day evaluation period commenced, and I continued the work of reviving what was waning in the small groups ministry. I met with the executive team and a member of the personnel team a couple of times, and they seemed encouraged by the progress I was making. I began to meet with Rick weekly, and our differences seem to melt into to common passions we had for reaching people. One part of the equation didn't change, however. I still felt exhausted at the end of each day.

This wasn't a satisfied exhaustion, one that you feel after the completion of a meaningful task. No, this was more of an exhaustion of a square peg trying to fit into a round hole. Though I was accomplishing what I set out to do, I was operating outside of my gifting as a believer and as a leader. When I had come on staff nearly eight years prior, my skills were celebrated. Now, though, the expressed need was to grow the ministry and its leadership. My strengths weren't minimized; the needs had just changed, and I wasn't feeling up to the task of meeting them over the long haul.

God was revealing more and more that He was leading me toward a new step of faith. My own heart was not leaping over the direction that my senior staff wanted small groups to go, even though I recognized the need. I felt like such a failure. One day, the answer became clear. I had taken my position as small groups pastor in 2006 because my skills helped to meet a need in our church. My skills were no longer the prominent needs, so what if...

In my heart of hearts, I had known within a week of the first meeting of the evaluation period what I felt like doing, but I knew the danger of responding quickly or emotionally. I waited, knowing that the Lord could confirm, repress, or replace what I was feeling. As the days turned into weeks, I didn't hear an audible voice from a burning bush, but my direction became clear. I would step aside from my position for the same reason I took it in the first place—for the good of the church. And it wasn't as if I couldn't look back nearly two years and see a new direction that God was already establishing in my life through a decades-old skill....

***

Philippians 1:6

And I am sure of this, that he who began a good work in you will bring it to completion at the day of Jesus Christ.

12 PLEASE EXIT THE RIDE

"After a period of prayer, evaluation, and discussion, I believe the time has come for me to resign my position as small groups pastor at Colonial Hills Church."

***

I first began to write publicly for the *Rankin County News* as a football stringer covering Rankin Academy (now defunct) football games as a seventh grader. My seventh grade English teacher had nothing to do with that gig, but Ms. Ann Knight had everything to do with my foundation as a writer. She taught me grammar skills that carried me through even my junior level college grammar class. My 11th grade English teacher, Ms. Leigh Ann Scharr, built on that foundation, noticing that I had a flair for writing and encouraging me to write.

Since high school, I wrote a few research papers—and one short story I wrote in the creative writing class I taught at Hernando High School over 20 years ago—but little else. (I saw one of my former students, whom I had not seen since he was in high school, at the gym recently. He brought back to my attention that long-forgotten short story.) I began to write some small group curriculum just before I became a pastor and continued that through the first few years in that role. However, something totally unexpected initiated a revival of my desire to write.

***

Tony and Tobie Pillstrom were in the process of adopting a little girl from China. They were among a handful of people who came together to begin an orphan care ministry in our church. When we were discussing strategies, Tobie practically insisted that I begin to blog. I knew what a blog was, even read a few from time to time, but I had never considered writing one. I took her up on her suggestion, though, and learned to blog. More than that, I began to write consistently.

I began writing once a week for our newly named 4theVoiceless blog, then twice a week. On three separate trips to Haiti, I took on the role of team storyteller. I loved observing the trip through the eyes of others and telling the stories when we returned. I found that finding different points of view came easily and that others were intrigued by how I could communicate their perspectives.

In the early fall of 2013, I began to feel a stirring toward reaching a wider audience with my blog. In writing about adoption and orphan care, I discovered that the most long-lasting solution to the world's orphan problems would ultimately come through strengthening families and stemming the tide of the problem at its roots. Having come from a healthy family myself—and understanding that *healthy* is a relative term when used to describe families—I felt a stirring to write about families and the legacy that families pass down through the stories they tell...and re-tell.

I had come to realize that the most fun my sisters and brother and I had when we were able to spend some time together was telling the same stories that we always told. We live several hours apart from one another now, so we usually see each other only a couple of times a year. Time is at a premium on our visits, but we always make time for the family stories. Our children are now mostly young adults, and they know our stories pretty well by now, too. I had never really given this much thought until 2013, when I decided to collect and tell our tales.

I can't even recall exactly when I started, but I wrote a few of our stories as blog posts as early as August of 2013. I call that my start date for a book I would title *Lines in the Gravel*, after one of our favorite family stories about learning to live at peace with one another. I was making steady progress on the book when I had an epiphany on the way home from our church staff's annual fall retreat in Grenada a month later. I had already met a time or two at that point with the team that would decide my professional fate within the next couple of months. I did not know before the retreat whether I wanted to stay or leave my staff position yet, but as planning for the 2014 calendar took place, I felt like an outsider looking in and that this would be my last staff retreat.

I had driven by myself, so I was considering direction for my life and ministry as I made the hour-and-a-half drive home. I thought about the possibilities of writing and speaking. I tend to be a dreamer but with a tendency toward the safe and easy route...at first. As thoughts of what could be welled up inside me this time, though, I felt certain that this was my calling. Just south of Senatobia, I felt three words impressed strongly on my spirit: family, story, legacy. I pulled into Wendy's a few minutes later to make sure that I typed the words into my Evernote app before they could escape. With that, I turned the corner and began to move toward a new dream.

I began to design my new blog and set the start date for it for November 4, 2013. I was still working through making sure that I was hearing from God when I met with Pastor Rick for one of our weekly meetings. At the conclusion of more than an hour of profitable conversation in his office on that Wednesday night in October, I felt the freedom to tell him of my decision. I followed up with a letter to senior staff and the personnel team the following week.

***

I worked hard to fulfill a promise I made in my resignation letter to serve the church body to the best of my ability in the succeeding months, right up until my very last day. I met once more with the team that had been evaluating me. They asked me how I wanted to transition out of my position, informing me that I had earned the right to go out on my own terms. I presented a list of my requests, all of which I had measured by the scant information I was able to gather on such matters and through counsel with a pastor on another church staff of similar size.

When I had settled on the decision to resign in October, I had told only my immediate family and two close friends. I had informed them of the importance of keeping the news very close to the vest. A timeline for my publicly stepping aside from my position was slow in coming. Though I felt restrained from moving forward, I was grateful to have a steady income for the Christmas season. When my family hosted the Christmas gathering for my side of the family, I broke the news to them.

Finally, on January 15, 2014, I was given a timeline of my

separation from our church staff. A flurry of meetings with various leaders and teams took place over the next two weeks, including an announcement to the church. The week after I packed the last of my belongings from my office, I served with a team from our church serving in Haiti. Three hectic months later, I was a published author.

***

What seemed like such a long period of time in late 2013 and early 2014 seems like just yesterday and many years ago at the same time now. I don't understand much of my last few months on the staff of my church. Perhaps I never will. My family continues to stay at our church, though I confess that I struggle at times to "stay well" as a former staff member; that can sometimes be rather awkward to me and to others.

I have to choose often to allow the Lord to take me "high on wings like eagles" and see the entire situation from His perspective: I was dissatisfied and not growing my ministry. God was working something different in me, equipping me and tugging me in another direction. I hate looking back and feeling that in the end I was unsuccessful in the position in which God had placed me. I must choose to be content that the work I couldn't accomplish is left for someone else to do. I must move toward what He wants me to do.

With the completion of this book, I will have told the majority of my life story, seen through the eyes of faith. Now, though, I am preparing to continue the exciting journey of helping others tell their stories that need to be captured. Stories of faith. Stories that matter. Stories that have the potential to impact generations like I pray mine will.

Some of the ideas that God has placed in my mind are breathtaking to me. I feel an urgency to equip others to be able to pass values from one generation to the next through the vehicle of story. I am reluctant to try to define what my ideas will look like all fleshed out. If could condense into one principle what I have learned from my roller coaster ride of faith, it is to follow God obediently—even when I don't understand—and quit trying to figure out what that looks like in my life. He gets to decide how He uses my obedience. Ultimately, that's for my good, for the good of others around me, and for His glory.

***

Psalm 56:11

In God I trust; I shall not be afraid. What can man do to me?

CONCLUSION

Since my trip to Disney World in 2007, I have not ridden another roller coaster. I have not been to another theme park or carnival or state fair. That's not to say I would never ride a roller coaster ever again in life; I just haven't created the opportunity. And I'm okay with that. You see, even with all the adventure and fun that a roller coaster can provide, I still prefer the safety and consistency of being upright and walking in the light with two feet on the ground.

I once had the idea that the Christian life, especially the sanctification part, meant that as I grew to understand the Lord and His principles more, my roller coaster faith life would flatten and straighten little by little until it was relatively smooth. I laugh at that notion now. I have since learned that a small, unexpected turn in life simply prepares me for a larger, more startling turn yet to come. Once I feel like I'm getting the hang of this thing called life, I'm reminded that I don't control it. I willingly gave God that control years ago.

***

A short and simple message at a school chapel service set the course for the urgency I feel when it comes to the spiritual legacy of my faith ride. I was a new teacher at a Christian school and new to school chapels, which can probably explain why I was paying

155

particular attention that day. A youth pastor from a local church was delivering the message, one crafted just for his junior high and high school audience.

That was 20 years ago, and I was 28 years old. In part of his message that day, the pastor asked the students of our school what they wanted said of them in 50 years. What legacy did they want for themselves? He began to reverse engineer his question, backing up 20 years, then 10, then five, then a single year. If you want to be known as a person of prayer, he offered, you wouldn't just wake up one day and become one. You had to start moving down that path now to arrive there then.

The words of that youth pastor gave focus to what had already been stirring inside of me. After all, "my" dream of a 40-year coaching career at one school was then on year six at school number three. Not exactly how I had drawn it up. Obviously, God had another plan for me, a plan that was more about who I become than what I accomplish. I have shared many of those stories with you throughout this book, but I wonder if you would give me time for one more. This one captured me during my family's celebration of Christmas 2013 and was a snapshot of legacy.

To give you a picture of what happened on Christmas, I must go back to when Dave Ramsey (the debt-free guy on the radio) came to our church. During all the sessions of his Financial Peace workshop, he worked us toward future financial freedom through discipline in the present. You may be familiar with his tag line: "Live like no one else so that, one day, you can live like no one else."

At the very end of his seminar, Ramsey challenged the seminar's participants to imagine what our church could become if we, as individuals, chose to live debt-free lives. He told us that we couldn't imagine how much we would be able to serve others if we would become debt-free as a church. He challenged us to "live like no one else so that, one day, you can *give* like no one else."

My family made the choice to live like that. The dream of exotic vacations and fancy houses and expensive sports cars has never been one that I have embraced. Don't get me wrong; I have my worldly desires (spring training in Florida with the Cardinals) just like anybody else. However, when Dave Ramsey says, "Live like no one else so that, one day, you can give like no one else," that charges me up like little else.

Years after that Dave Ramsey conference, I was driving into town one day for a reason that I do not recall. I flipped the radio over to the Dave Ramsey Show to listen for my ten-minute drive. This was during the Christmas season, so Ramsey had been focused on the giving aspect of his financial plan. That day, I was immediately captured by an interview he did with a man known theretofore theretofore as Secret Santa. This was a guy who would go to different cities around the country around Christmas time each year, dressed as Santa, and give away thousands of dollars in one hundred-dollar bills to people who looked like they needed some hope. He told his backstory of receiving such hope himself at a small-town Mississippi diner years earlier and paying it forward for the rest of his life.

I'm not the type of Christ-follower prone to visions, but right there in my truck, I had a vision as plain as the nose on my face. Every Christmas from my childhood into my young adulthood, my grandfather would sit and watch as all the presents were distributed and opened. When he was sure that they were all opened, he would slowly lift his hunched 6'3" frame from his chair and walk around to each grandchild, handing out envelopes as he moved around the room. We all knew what to expect in those plain, white envelopes: one ten-dollar bill. His gift to us.

I remember that I was about halfway to my destination when I saw myself one day as a grandfather at Christmas. I saw my family gathered at our house on Christmas Eve, laughing, loving, singing, and exchanging gifts. Afterward, I saw myself rising from my chair to walk around the room. Each person who came would get an envelope, and each person would know what to expect in it: one

one-hundred-dollar bill. When everyone had their money, we would go outside, get in our vehicles, and go give the money away.

That vision was so crystal clear that I knew I would do it one day. One day. Oh, those words are the hallmark of good intentions that are never realized. They are the basis for *rollover days*. The warm feeling of "one day" collected urgency as I made another turn toward town. In that short little stretch before my next turn, the still, small voice of God reminded me of a principle I had learned in that chapel service in 1994. I might not be able to give $100 each to a house full of people yet, but we did have $75 that we had set aside for our family's gift to Jesus that Christmas. (It is His birthday, after all. Who goes to a birthday party to give gifts to everyone BUT the birthday boy?) Not only that, but there were just the five of us. "One day" suddenly became that year!

***

A few days before Christmas, my family went out to dinner and a movie to enjoy some time together and to purposefully give away a ten- and a five-dollar bill apiece. Drew, our youngest, would have probably been about three or four years old then. As we waited in line at the concession stand at the movie theater, Drew tapped me on the leg and said, "I want to give my money to him." He pointed back to the lanky African-American teenager who was taking up tickets. He decided to give him his ten and marched alone back across the lobby. Reaching the young man, Drew tapped him on the leg, held his money out, and said, "Merry Christmas." The young man looked at Drew, and then scanned the lobby for validation. Seeing us looking his way, he sent an "is this legit?" look our way. I responded with a thumbs up, and he reached down and hugged Drew.

We have developed some great memories giving away our Jesus money. Loretta elicited a smile from the only young girl working at Wendy's one night. (Oh, there were other employees present, but she appeared to be the only one actually *working*.) Garrett and I anonymously paid for the meal of a family behind us at Chick Fil A one year and were able to see the astonished look on the dad's face when he turned to tell the rest of his family that someone has paid for their meal. Before we left that day, we went to the restroom, where our friend Tyler was bagging the trash. He was the one who had earlier taken our order and sworn silence on who was paying for the meal. He told us that what we hadn't seen a few minutes later was the dad walking back to the counter, slapping down some money and saying, "Well, if he can do it, then I can, too." And he blessed someone else that day.

***

Now, fast forward to Christmas Day 2013. The usual progression of the day was a big lunch, the reading of the Christmas story, and the exchanging of gifts. This was also the day that I would be making the big announcement that I would be stepping aside from my church staff position to pursue writing and speaking full time. Another faith move. I had begun the Family Story Legacy blog less than two months before and had been working on *Lines in the Gravel* for about four months, so there may have been hints of my new direction but nothing concrete until the Christmas Day announcement. (Note: The Family Story Legacy blog has now morphed into the Values Storying blog at www.alainsworth.com—be sure to check it out.)

After I broke the news to my family, the Lord confirmed my new direction in the sweetest way. My niece, Alison, also had an announcement to make. She had not yet established church membership since leaving home for college at the University of Arkansas. She had, however, continued to set aside her tithe money and felt that the Lord was moving her to give it before the end of the year. She just didn't know where.

After reading the account of my Secret Santa vision on my blog a week or two before Christmas, she came up with a plan. She announced that each of us would give away her money for her. She gave us the choice of giving to organizations with which she had been involved or by writing in an organization of our own

159

choosing. As I quickly wrote in "House of Abraham—Jacmel, Haiti," I was undone.

I was undone because of my sweet niece's response to the Lord's prompting in her heart. Undone because as soon as I took the first step toward making the Lord's direction in my life public, He allowed me to see an object lesson of legacy immediately. Undone because even though I am still a far cry from becoming the guy who hands out $100 to everybody at Christmas, the Lord is still moving my family to give. Undone because my words moved someone else to respond to Jesus. Undone that the writing ability that He gave me was used to bless Him in return. Undone because if my family who knows me best was on board with my faith move, I knew I would have the advantage of starting with a core group of supporters who wouldn't abandon me. Undone that values already several generations deep in our family were manifesting themselves through the latest generation.

***

I define the foundation of my platform through the term *values storying*, the passing along of values from one generation to the next through the stories we tell...and re-tell. I'm concerned about what I'm seeing happen to the legacies of those who pass from this life into the next. No matter how good or bad a life someone lived, there are always lessons to be learned from his or her life. But many of these life stories are being lost.

One of the most neglected disciplines—even in lives of faith— is reflection. Where am I? How did I get here? Do I like the direction I'm going? What needs to change? And what do I need to do to make those changes?

With the hectic pace of life in the 21st century, when do people take the time to remember and reflect? Not for nostalgia's sake but for legacy's sake. For the good of the next generation, not just our own. For life that will go on after our immortality becomes reality. The foundation statement for my whole platform of values storying is this: Nostalgia reaches into the past with both hands to try to grasp what is gone and likely never will be again. Legacy, on the other hand, reaches into the past with one hand to grasp what is teachable and passes it forward with the other hand to the next generation. And story is the primary vehicle for the handing down of our values.

***

An interesting study in regard to legacy is the evolution of how a person's death is remembered. Not too many decades ago, a dead person's body would lie at his or her home for about a week while loved ones came to visit and spend time with the surviving family. Family would even "sit up" with the body (which was fertile ground for some hilariously funny stories, but I digress). As time went on, funeral homes hosted the body for a couple of days' visitation before the funeral. Today, more often than not, the visitation for a funeral is a couple of hours before the funeral. I have officiated a number of funerals where the prevailing sentiment seemed to be, "Well, we felt like we needed to do something." Often, nowadays, bodies are cremated, and a memorial service is put together when it is convenient for friends and family.

What does this say about the grieving process? What does is say about our ability to remember and reflect? What does is say about the value of life and legacy?

So many athletes have gone on to play in games after the death of a close friend or family member because that loved one "would have wanted it that way." I have (not so) jokingly told my family that I want my body to lie in state for a week or so to give everyone who wants to visit appropriate time. I want anyone who wants to give a testimony of how my life impacted his or hers to have the opportunity to do so. Any ball games in which my kids or (one day) grandkids are involved—well, I want them NOT to play, and I want the games to be cancelled because "I would have wanted it that way." I'm just letting them know ahead of time so that they won't justify what "Dad would have wanted." I want people who would mourn my death to have adequate time to contemplate because I have experienced the change that often comes through reflection.

One day, I will step off of the ride of faith for good. My faith will become sight. In addition to seeing my Savior face-to-face and enjoying all the fruits of Heaven, I will also give an account. Like so many others, my accomplishments will fall far short of even what I wished I could have accomplished as a follower of Jesus. But that won't be the time for urgency. Time will have already slipped into eternity for me. Opportunities to boldly step out and follow God, even when the rest of the world thinks I'm crazy, will have passed. So, too, opportunities to encourage, inspire, and challenge others through my faith stories will have passed.

***

What stories are you passing along as treasure to the next generation? Think about where you live, where you work, where you go to school, where you play. There are those behind you in many spheres of your life who would benefit from your stories and, more than that, from the values they contain. Good stories and bad. Happy stories and sad. Stories of times you responded well to your circumstances and those in which you blew it. Stories of victory and those of defeat. And especially stories of faith.

Your stories are a gift. You have a collection of stories that are unique among all the people who have ever lived. They are not given to be safeguarded but to be shared so that the next generation will know. Story begets story. You have now read mine (thanks) and undoubtedly been reminded of some of your own stories that matter. The time for urgency in making them known to others is now, even while you are still riding the roller coaster in your own faith life. Especially now. The next generation is desperately counting on you to tell your stories from your ride of faith so that they are pointed toward Jesus. I'm counting on you to speak up. And so are they.

***

Revelation 19:11-16

Then I saw heaven opened, and behold, a white horse! The one sitting on it is called Faithful and True, and in righteousness he judges and makes war. His eyes are like a flame of fire, and on his head are many diadems, and he has a name written that no one knows but himself. He is clothed in a robe dipped in blood, and the name by which he is called is The Word of God. And the armies of heaven, arrayed in fine linen, white and pure, were following him on white horses. From his mouth comes a sharp sword with which to strike down the nations, and he will rule them with a rod of iron. He will tread the winepress of the fury of the wrath of God the Almighty. On his robe and on his thigh he has a name written, King of kings and Lord of lords.

EPILOGUE

When I began chronicling my faith stories, I began to notice that my family's needs seemed to multiply. One day, a thought occurred to me as I was jotting as many notes for the epilogue of the book as for the book itself. In the process of writing a book on faith stories, financial pressures and health issues threatened to cause our family to unravel. But, I thought, why wouldn't they? I wasn't writing this book in a bubble. Why wouldn't the process of writing the book turn into a faith story of its own?

Hand in hand with every need, though, was God's provision for us in often unexpected, unpredictable ways. He has reminded us frequently that He is not only the source of our provision but that He *is* our provision. That's the essence of my stories from the roller coaster ride of faith, stories that my family will tell...and re-tell about God's faithfulness. My roller coaster ride of faith is still very much an unfinished story. I'll continue to tell my stories as they happen. Won't you join me and tell yours, too?

Let me help you get started. Check out the following website, where you can submit a short version of your faith story: **www.whativaluemost.com**. You can find my story there along with many other examples. Each story is 400 words or fewer. If you would like to know how to step onto the roller coaster ride of faith in Jesus Christ, you can discover that there, as well.

DELETED SCENES

Editing my work is one of my least favorite parts of the writing process. In addition to finding mistakes that a former English teacher just should not make, I have to cut parts of the book that don't quite fit or would cause the reader to become distracted. But those are good stories that should be told!

I would love to send you some of the deleted scenes from Stories from the *Roller Coaster (of a Faith Life)* and some of the detailed accounts of how God tested my family's faith even while I was writing this book. If you would like to receive those stories, simply attach a copy of your receipt for the purchase of this book to a blank email with "Deleted Scenes" in the subject line, and send it to **rollercoasterdeletedscenes@gmail.com.**

ABOUT THE AUTHOR

Al Ainsworth is a writer and speaker who focuses on "values storying," the use of the vehicle of story to pass along values to the next generation—whether the next generation of family, employees, students, or church members. Through careers in teaching, coaching, and pastoring, he has prepared others for the next phases of their lives through the values that he often relates through his unique style of storytelling. He is the author of *Lines in the Gravel (and 52 Other Re-Told Childhood Tales)*.

Al lives with his wife, Loretta, and their three children—Ashton, Garrett, and Drew—in Hernando, Mississippi.

▪ ▪

Al writes regularly at his Values Storying blog at www.alainsworth.com.

Contact him through his speaker's page at www.alainsworth.com.

▪ ▪

Made in the USA
San Bernardino, CA
17 November 2014